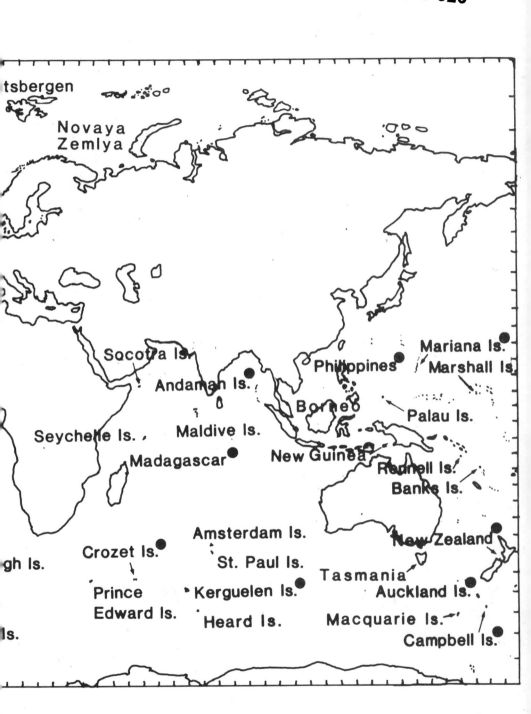

tsbergen

Novaya
Zemlya

Socotra Is.

Andaman Is.

Philippines

Mariana Is.

Marshall Is.

Borneo

Palau Is.

Seychelle Is.

Maldive Is.

Madagascar

New Guinea

Rennell Is.

Banks Is.

Amsterdam Is.

Crozet Is.

gh Is.

St. Paul Is.

New Zealand

Prince
Edward Is.

Kerguelen Is.

Tasmania

Auckland Is.

Heard Is.

Macquarie Is.

Campbell Is.

Is.

BELOIT COLLEGE LIBRARIES

The Island Waterfowl

The Island Waterfowl

MILTON W. WELLER

Iowa State University Press / AMES, IOWA, U.S.A.

MILTON W. WELLER is Professor and Head, Department of Entomology, Fisheries, and Wildlife, University of Minnesota. His specialization is in waterfowl (ducks, geese, and swans) and the ecology and management of their wetland habitats. He has conducted field work in North America, South America, New Zealand, Australia, Great Britain, and Antarctica and on isolated southern hemisphere and tropical islands.

Composed and printed by The Iowa State University Press, Ames, Iowa 50010

First edition, 1980

Library of Congress Cataloging in Publication Data

Weller, Milton Webster.
    The island waterfowl.

    Bibliography: p.
    Includes index.
    1. Anatidae.   2. Island fauna.   I. Title.
QL696.A52W44   598.4′1′045   79-24016
ISBN 0-8138-1310-7

C O N T E N T S

P R E F A C E

FEW FAMILIES of birds are more widely distributed or better adapted to diverse climatic conditions than waterfowl. Perhaps best known are those able to utilize resources at high latitudes by long-distance migration between breeding and wintering areas. Such exceptional powers of flight and the natural expansion of successful populations have resulted in visitation and often establishment of such waterfowl on suitable land masses wherever there is fresh water and food. Isolated islands are no exception, and the ornithological literature is full of reports of potentially pioneering accidentals on even the most remote oceanic islands. If conditions are suitable and establishment occurs, such islands eventually may serve as breeding areas, with a postbreeding movement to an adjacent continent for winter. But in the most remote areas or where wind direction and severe weather dictate, migration is impractical and birds must be able to reside in these areas year-round or they do not survive. Such is the case of the endemic ducks of certain remote islands in the "Roaring Forties" and "Furious Fifties" of the southern hemisphere. Not only are these birds dramatic examples of pioneering and adaptation to areas with severe climate but the evolutionary consequences of this isolation give clues to the function of common biological characters of continental waterfowl otherwise taken for granted. It was fascination for these hardy, isolated, and often solitary endemics that resulted in my interest in waterfowl that reside on islands.

In my initial effort to examine the ducks of remote islands, it was necessary to review their distribution, taxonomic status, and population level. Because of the presence of endemic ducks on remote tropical islands as well as subantarctic islands, the warmer location seemed more logical for study. But human pressures have so influenced the population status of such tropical species that this research seemed less likely to yield meaningful results. Populations of ducks of south temperate or subantarctic islands either were larger and easier to study or their numbers were unknown, thus warranting investigation. However, some of the islands were impossible to reach without the facilities of a major expedition, and this need for logistic support eventually led me to the National Science Foundation Office of Polar Programs.

Many islands have more than one species of waterfowl; and by comparing islands with various numbers of species, we gain insight into the evolution of waterfowl-faunal complexes on larger islands or even continents. Faunal change occurs constantly, as discussed by several authors (Terborgh and Faaborg 1973, Lynch and Johnson 1974). It was, therefore, a unique and meaningful experience when we discovered the first breeding population of Speckled Teal (*Anas flavirostris*) on the remote island of South Georgia, formerly inhabited by only one anatid, the pintail *Anas g. georgica* (Weller and Howard 1972). What interspecific pressures will result, and what new division of space, food, and other resources will be necessary for the survival of this second species? Will it survive and, if so, will a third species arrive and work its way into the system?

Results of field work on five archipelagoes have been reported elsewhere (Weller 1972, 1974, 1975a, 1975c, 1975d); this summary is an attempt to synthesize both unpublished and published observations with the work of others to consider the following issues:

- What are the endemic island ducks, where are they found, and how do they differ from their living relatives? (The reader can skip this section if knowledgeable about the forms or more inclined to look at possible explanations for their occurrence.)
- What are the characteristics of potential pioneering species, and what factors influence their colonization?
- How have birds that seemingly evolved as freshwater species adapted to oceanic islands?
- What changes occur in reproductive behavior in solitary island ducks?
- Why are the endemic island waterfowl restricted to certain tropical, southern cold-temperate, or subantarctic islands?
- How does island speciation and island pioneering relate to faunal development and resource allocation in more complex anatid groupings?
- What is the status of each of these forms of endemic waterfowl and how can we ensure their survival?

By necessity and by design this summary raises more questions than it answers. It is hoped that some readers will find sufficient fascination to further examine these and related issues about island waterfowl.

A C K N O W L E D G M E N T S

THE FIELD WORK that produced some of the observations reported here and the resultant summary could not have been possible without the help of many individuals and organizations. My wife Doris not only aided me in the field, laboratory, and office but understood my goals when I needed to be away island-hopping for long periods.

Many persons in major organizations facilitated the program: Dr. George A. Llano, former program manager for biology in the Office of Polar Programs, National Science Foundation, understood the importance of subantarctic islands in interpreting the biology of the Antarctic. Much of the work was done under NSF grants GV-21491 and GV-35430 to Iowa State University and OPP 76-20058 to the University of Minnesota. Sir Vivian Fuchs and Dr. Richard M. Laws, directors (in sequence) of the British Antarctic Survey, made numerous arrangements to facilitate my research. Dr. Gordon R. Williams, director of the New Zealand Wildlife Service, aided in organizational matters and shared a tent on the Auckland Islands. A number of persons at Iowa State University helped take care of many of my duties during my long absences, especially Dr. Kenneth Carlander, Dr. Roger Bachman, and Dr. Oscar Tauber. Fred Kent of the University of Iowa Photo Service provided advice and assistance in photography and processing that much enhanced my photographic recording of these islands and their birds.

In addition to those mentioned above, numerous individuals, agency representatives, and local residents assisted in various ways on each island, or provided arrangements and advice for getting there.

- *Tierra del Fuego*—Tom and Natalie Goodall (Estancia Harberton), Adrian and Stefanie Goodall, T. R. Bridges (Estancia Viamonte), and Dr. Philip S. Humphrey (University of Kansas).
- *Falkland Islands*—My field assistant, Maurice Rumboll, field party member Dr. John R. Baker of Iowa State University, Mr. and Mrs. James Clement (Falkland Islands Co.-Fitzroy), Mr. and Mrs. Alan Miller (Port San Carlos), Richard Cockwell (Fox Bay East), Mr. and Mrs. Rod Napier (West Point Island), Ian Strange (resident naturalist), Mr. and Mrs. D. G. B. King (Upland Goose Hotel),

M. Bound (assistant colonial secretary), John Bound (Postal Service), Colonial Secretary and acting Governor J. A. Jones and his wife, Tedd Clapp and his staff of the British Antarctic Survey, George Betz (field assistant and driver), Daniel Borland (Meteorological Service), and the late Ian Campbell (Air Service). John Faaborg assisted in laboratory work and Dr. and the late Mrs. Sewall Pettingil provided information and advice.

• *South Georgia*—My field assistant Robert L. Howard, R. Chinn (station leader), Dr. Peter Tilbrook (scientific leader), and Captain Tom Woodfield and the fine crew of the *R. R. S. Bransfield*. Dr. W. L. N. Tickell provided helpful suggestions.

• *New Zealand and the Auckland Islands*—Expedition leader Brian D. Bell and expedition members R. Nilsson and R. Russ; Captain A. Black of the *R. V. Acheron*; Harry Simmons, Bill Heaply, and others of the NSF Office at Christchurch; U.S. expedition member Dr. Peter Connors (University of California, Berkeley); K. J. Westerskov (Otago University), R. W. Balham (Victoria University).

• *Hawaii*—Henry Hansen, Eugene Kridler, Vernon Byrd, and John Sincock of the U.S. Fish and Wildlife Service; Paul Banko of the U.S. National Park Service; Ah Fat and Barbara Lee and Tom Telford of the Hawaii Division of Fish and Game.

Museums, collections of live birds, and certain libraries have been very valuable in gathering data and gaining insights on island waterfowl. Collections and curators are as follows: Dr. David W. Snow (British Museum of Natural History-Tring), Dr. Dean Amadon and Dr. Wesley Lanyon (American Museum of Natural History), Dr. George Watson and Dr. Richard Zusi (U.S. National Museum of Natural History), Dr. Jean Prevost (Muséum National d'Histoire Naturelle, Paris), Dr. G. Mauersberger (Museum für Naturkunde der Humboldt-Uni, DDR, Berlin), Bengt-Olav Stolt (Naturhistoriska Riksmuseet, Stockholm), Dr. Jean Delacour (Cléres, France), Dr. Janet Kear and Dr. Geoffrey Matthews (The Wildfowl Trust, Slimbridge, England), Dr. F. Salomonsen (Zoologisk Museum, Copenhagen), N. J. Ytrebert (Zoological Laboratory, University of Oslo), Dr. P. J. Olney (Zoological Society of London), Dr. Euan Dunn (Edward Grey Institute of Field Ornithology, Oxford University).

Several people have read, commented on, and supplemented the text in a most helpful manner, but I must assume responsibility for errors or failure to recognize their intentions: Dr. Frank Bellrose, Dr. Richard Crawford, Dr. John Faaborg, Dr. Leigh Fredrickson, Dr. James Karr, Dr. Janet Kear, and Dr. Frank McKinney as well as Nancy Bohlen and other editors at the Iowa State University Press. Pamela Dykstra did the final typing, and Alan Afton aided with statistical analyses.

The Island Waterfowl

Distribution and Characteristics of Island Forms

ALTHOUGH my original interests centered around endemic waterfowl that are the sole resident anatid on an island, are sufficiently distinct to have been viewed as taxonomic entities, and reside on small and remote islands or archipelagoes, it was difficult to delineate birds with these characteristics. As a result it seemed advantageous to examine sedentary, endemic waterfowl of all land masses other than major continents. These island waterfowl can be arranged by degree of taxonomic differentiation (subspecies, semispecies, species, etc.) and by degree of geographic isolation from other ducks (i.e., whether solitary or part of a complex).

Many forms are only racially distinct and often use the same geographic areas as other species of waterfowl (Table 1.1). Most of these races will be considered only as they relate to patterns of isolation and differentiation. Table 1.2 lists the more distinctive forms, including semispecies, species, and genera. Some are the only anatid on an island (hence they may have nonoverlapping or allopatric distributions), or they may be one of several species occurring in the same geographic area (sympatric distributions). All these distinctive forms are treated in "species" accounts starting with the least differentiated (and presumably most recent isolates) to the well-differentiated forms, including distinctive genera. Although some species are illustrated in this text, the reader is referred to taxonomic reviews for illustrations of all species (Delacour 1954–64, Johnsgard 1978, Todd 1979).

Every possible degree of genetic differentiation seems to be represented by island waterfowl, and differences in handling taxonomic terminology for such isolates complicates making an array from least to most differentiated. A few forms are clearly unique species or genera, but most are semispecies—either recent isolates or forms that have not changed rapidly and that are geographically isolated so their species status remains untested. Early taxonomists tended to dramatize even small differences with distinctive terminology, whereas the current trend is to use subspecific rank to demonstrate recent origin and relationships,

TABLE 1.1
Resident island subspecies usually sympatric with
other breeding waterfowl, arranged taxonomically

East Indian Wandering Whistling Duck (*Dendrocygna a. arcuata*)
Lesser Wandering Whistling Duck (*D. a. pygmaea*)
Vancouver Canada Goose (*Branta canadensis fulva*)
Falkland Upland Sheldgoose (*Chloëphaga picta leucoptera*)
Falkland Kelp Sheldgoose (*C. hybrida malvinarum*)
Moluccan Radjah Shelduck (*Tadorna r. radjah*)
Aleutian Green-winged Teal (*Anas crecca nimia*)
East Indian Gray Teal (*A. g. gibberifrons*)
Rennell Gray Teal (*A. g. remissa*)
Greenland Mallard (*A. platyrhynchos conboschas*)
New Zealand Gray Duck (*A. s. superciliosa*)
Palau Gray Duck (*A. s. pelewensis*)
New Zealand Shoveler (*A. rhynchotis variegata*)
Banks White-eye (*Aythya australis extima*)
Faeroe Eider (*Somateria mollissima faeroeensis*)
Greenland Red-breasted Merganser (*Mergus serrator schioleri*)
Madagascar White-backed Duck (*Thalassornis leuconotus insularis*)

Note: Terminology modified from Johnsgard 1978.

TABLE 1.2
Resident island waterfowl either allopatric or distinctive taxa sympatric with
other breeding waterfowl, from least (subspp.) to most differentiated (genera)

ALLOPATRIC TAXA

Galapagos Pintail (*Anas bahamensis galapagensis*)
Washington or Coues's Gadwall (*A. strepera couesi*)
Indian Ocean Pintail (*A. acuta eatoni* and *A. a. drygalskii*)
Laysan Teal (*A. platyrhynchos laysanensis*)
Mariana Mallard (*A. p. oustaleti*)

SYMPATRIC FORMS

Andaman Teal (*Anas gibberifrons albogularis*)
Madagascar or Bernier's Teal (*A. bernieri*)
South Georgia Pintail (*A. g. georgica*)
Hawaiian Duck (*A. platyrhynchos wyvilliana*)
Meller's Duck (*A. melleri*)
Madagascar White-eye (*Aythya innotata*)
Falkland Flightless Steamer Duck (*Tachyeres brachypterus*)
Flightless Teal (*Anas a. aucklandica* and *A. a. nesiotis*)
Brown Teal (*A. aucklandica chlorotis*)
New Zealand Shelduck (*Tadorna variegata*)
Philippine Duck (*A. luzonica*)
Cuban or Black-billed Whistling Duck (*Dendrocygna arborea*)
Spotted Whistling Duck (*D. guttata*)
Auckland Merganser (*Mergus australis*) (extinct)
New Zealand Scaup (*Aythya novae-seelandiae*)
Salvadori's Duck (*Anas [= Salvadorina] waiguiensis*)
Hawaiian Goose (*Branta sandvicensis*)
Blue Mountain Duck (*Hymenolaimus malacorhynchos*)

especially when island isolates do not overlap with closely related forms. Greenway's (1958) terminology epitomizes the problem that biologists have had in reference to island species, when in one book he lists the Laysan Teal as *Anas platyrhynchos laysanensis* (p. 10), suggesting a direct Mallard (*A. platyrhynchos*) origin; *A. wyvilliana laysanensis* (p. 50), implying derivation from the Hawaiian Duck (*A. platyrhynchos wyvilliana*); and *A. laysanensis* (p. 167). Scientific terminology used in this text is from Delacour (1954, 1956, 1959, 1964), as modified by Johnsgard (1965). Where possible, English names based on islands will be used to avoid either taxonomic or evolutionary implications but the word island will be deleted to avoid redundant or inconsistent terminology.

Major islands discussed are shown on the endpaper map with major endemics indicated by dots. It can be seen from the map that island endemics are most prevalent in the tropics and on southern cold-temperate and subantarctic islands.

Not all island forms are sedentary (Table 1.3), and those that do migrate often have clear-cut wintering areas as well (Fig. 1.1). However, the migratory status of a number of island forms is not known. Presumably, genetic isolation of migratory forms may be maintained by geographic isolation on wintering areas as well as breeding areas. These forms will not be dealt with in detail here, but the subject was reviewed by Salomonsen (1955). It is significant that the migratory island waterfowl are all geese characterized by strong family ties. They breed in Arctic areas and form distinctive races or semispecies. The Pink-footed Goose (*Anser fabalis brachyrhynchus*) often has been regarded as a separate species. With the exception of the Greenland White-fronted Goose (*A. albifrons flavirostris*) all inhabit several major islands of similar ecological type; the Pink-footed Goose uses widely separated islands—Greenland, Iceland, and Spitsbergen. Greenway (1958) suggested that the extinct Labrador Duck (*Camptorhynchus labradorius*) may have nested on small islands off the northeastern coast of North America, but its migratory behavior is unknown.

Fossil anatids will not be discussed in any detail, but a number of large and unique island forms existed (Howard 1975, Olson and Wet-

TABLE 1.3
Migratory waterfowl that breed on islands or archipelagoes
but winter in restricted areas and maintain distinctive populations

Pink-footed Goose (*Anser fabalis brachyrhynchus*)
Aleutian Canada Goose (*Branta canadensis leucopareia*)
Greenland White-fronted Goose (*A. albifrons flavirostris*)
Greater Snow Goose (*A. caerulescens atlanticus*)
Barnacle Goose (*B. leucopsis*)
Ruddy-headed Sheldgoose (*Chloëphaga rubidiceps*)

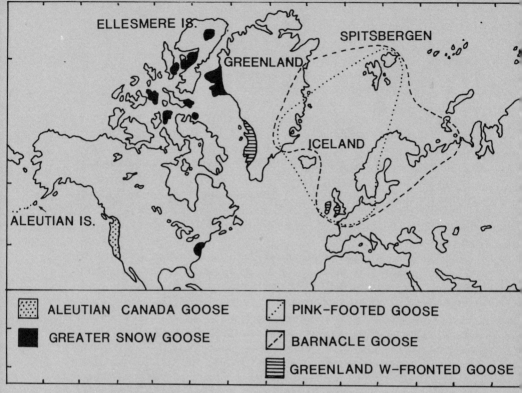

Fig. 1.1. Breeding (northern islands) and wintering areas (southern islands or continents) of some migratory island geese.

more 1976). An accurate accounting of these might allow an analysis of faunal equilibrium, including colonization and extinction, on each archipelago—a topic of considerable interest (Diamond 1969, Lynch and Johnson 1974, Abbott and Grant 1976).

The following brief descriptions of island waterfowl emphasize distribution, taxonomic relationships of potential parental stock or near relatives, plumages, and status. The emphasis on plumage (sometimes of assumed parental stock as well) is essential because changes in degree of sexual dichromatism, distinctiveness of color patterns, and seasonal dichromatism are common in island isolates. Details of plumages and plumage cycles in ducks are discussed in Chapter 3, but it is necessary here to review the dramatic changes in island waterfowl to which the reader should be alerted in the following descriptions. Terms used to describe various body parts and feather tracts are given in Fig. 1.2.

All ducks seem to have two plumages annually. In northern hemisphere ducks males are brighter than females (sexual dichromatism), but males have bright plumages (nuptial or alternate) only during the winter and prebreeding period and are dull during the summer molt period (eclipse, nonnuptial, or basic plumage). This is termed seasonal dichromatism. In some tropical or subtropical forms there is little or no difference in these plumages seasonally or between sexes. Usually some other sexual dimorphism is apparent such as larger size and more distinctive voices in males. A common misconception is that tropical and south-temperate anatids all lack bright patterns or sexual dichromatism. Some do, but others have dramatic sexual dichromatism and lack the seasonal dichromatism common to most northern hemisphere species (i.e., permanent dichromatism).

Island isolates that originated from dichromatic northern forms have provided insight into the function of plumages and plumage change. In general the island forms have lost dramatic sexual dichromatism in the males and often are darker in both sexes. The loss of distinct vermiculations and crossbarring of feathers of males is commonplace. In most cases some evidence of general plumage pattern or feather pattern remains to demonstrate evolutionary origins. The result

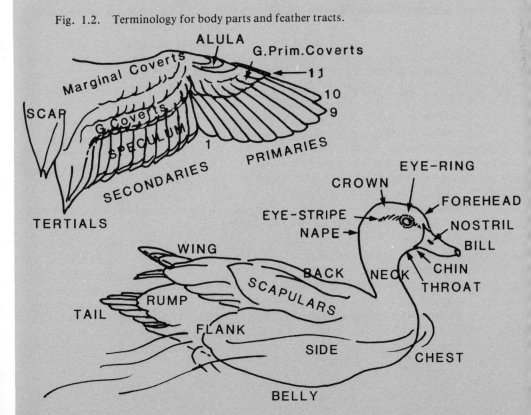

Fig. 1.2. Terminology for body parts and feather tracts.

is that males of island species in breeding plumage often resemble the dull, nonbreeding or eclipse plumage of northern hemisphere males. Males of island species in nonbreeding plumage are quite henlike, and there is much confusion in the literature and on museum specimen labels as to sex identification. Other island forms have had their origins from parental stock with little or no dimorphism. The resulting birds retain most of these parental characters but typically are darker in color and smaller in body size and have appendages of reduced size.

Galapagos Pintail

The Galapagos Pintail (*Anas bahamensis galapagensis*) is similar to its obvious ancestor, the White-cheeked or Bahama Pintail of South America (*A. bahamensis*). It is satisfactorily represented by subspecific status; but its reduced size, subdued colors, and isolation on the Galapagos Islands induced Ridgeway (1890) to consider it a full species. It is one of few island forms that seemingly arose by isolation from westward movement from its source area. It is the only resident anatid on the Galapagos Islands, and few species of waterfowl seem to reach there as accidentals. The Blue-winged Teal (*A. discors*) has been recorded most (Gifford 1913, Leveque et al. 1966, Harris 1974).

Like the other Neotropical pintails, Galapagos Pintails are essentially sexually monochromatic and also lack the vermiculated feathers in males common to northern Pintails (*A. acuta*). However, sexes differ in voice and differ slightly in size and in brilliance of bill and speculum color. The Galapagos Pintail is slightly smaller and less elongate than either the continental race (*A. b. rubrirostris*) of the White-cheeked Pintail or the race found on the Bahama Islands (*A. b. bahamensis*) (Delacour 1956). The white throat tends to be duller, and the facial area is flecked with brown, making the demarcation between the brown crown, the eye-stripe, and the white facial throat less distinct (Scott 1960). The upperparts are generally darker in color with less buff edging, especially on the tertials. The underparts have less pinkish cast to the brown. Spotting of the chest and ventral surfaces is more obscure due to less definite spots and a darker background. The red sides of the bill, especially in females, seem to be less brilliant than in White-cheeked Pintails. The speculum is almost identical to that of White-cheeked Pintails, but the scapulars and tertials of males are less colorful in the Galapagos Islands race. Most of these characters are reminiscent of juvenile females of the continental race. Sexes can be difficult to distinguish, but the speculum of males tends to be more brilliant due especially to the more rufous margin that contrasts with the black-tipped green speculum. Seasonal differences in plumages, if present, are not conspicuous. Downy young do not differ noticeably from the continental race.

Galapagos Pintails are widespread but not common on at least the nine major islands and are generally very tame (Gifford 1913). They are seen on the saline lagoons where they feed with American Flamingos (*Phoenicopterus ruber*), and they may even rear their young there (Gifford 1913, Beebe 1924). However, they also use freshwater ponds or seasonally flooded pools and, occasionally, quiet marine coves. A freshwater lake had formed in the volcano that constitutes most of the island of Fernadina (Moore 1978), and many pintails were thought to have perished in the eruption of 1968 (Kear and Williams 1978). Gifford (1913) recorded protective behavior by broody hens and the presence of the male as well as the female with at least one brood. He also noted broods in both March and August, suggesting double rearing periods or an extended nesting period. Harris (1974) suggested that the birds breed whenever conditions are suitable.

Although the islands are 1.8 to 3 million years old (Bailey 1976), most of the present surfaces were formed from volcanic eruptions in Pleistocene to recent times (Cox 1966, Williams 1966). One can only assume that pintails have reached the island since the origin of the wetlands that appear to have existed for the last 10,000 years (Colinvaux 1968).

Washington or Coues's Gadwall

The Washington Gadwall (*Anas strepera couesi*) is an extinct subspecies known only from two specimens now in the U.S. National Museum. It was found on Washington Island at about lat. 4° N. Unfortunately, the specimens are poor and in uncertain plumages; little can be added to descriptions by Streets (1877), Phillips (1923), and Delacour (1956). The single male specimen may be subadult, but it appears to have an eclipselike plumage lacking the extensive vermiculations, blackish undertail, and colorful wing of northern Gadwall (*A. s. strepera*) males. It does have a few vermiculated feathers and considerable barring and is generally brown. The hen is like a diminutive Gadwall female but with a drab, juvenilelike wing (Phillips 1923). Greenway (1958) questioned whether these were true endemics or merely young of some injured Gadwalls that remained and nested. However, the plumage characters of the two specimens compare favorably with changes noted in other island isolates—reduced size and brightness and loss of vermiculated feathering of males. Moreover, Ripley (1957) pointed out what may have been an important adaptation—an increased number of bill lamellae that could influence their food-size selection.

The form presumably could have arisen from isolates of either North American or Asiatic Gadwalls. Gadwalls do occasionally migrate to the Hawaiian Islands (Berger 1972), but their source is not known. Yocum (1964) reported Gadwalls in the Marshall Islands west of Washington Island at about lat. 10° S. Ripley (Greenway 1958) reported an apparent nesting by Gadwall on the Tuamotu Islands southeast of Washington Island.

According to Streets (1877) Gadwalls used the unique perched lake and associated peat bog on Washington Island (Hutchinson 1950). After consultation with a former resident of Washington Island, Wetmore (1925) concluded that this form may not have been recognized because of other migrant waterfowl. Waterfowl hunting, he suggested, may have been responsible for its extinction.

Indian Ocean Pintails

The Indian Ocean Pintails of the Kerguelen Islands (*Anas acuta eatoni*) and the Crozet Islands (*A. a. drygalskii*) seem to be relatively recent isolates of the dramatically sexually dichromatic northern Pintail. The Kerguelen form originally was named a full species, the Eaton's Teal (*Querquedula eatoni* Sharpe 1875). Salvadori (1895) later recognized its pintail-like features and placed it in the genus *Dafila* once used for all pintails. The Crozet form was named *A. drygalskii* by Reichenow (1904). Falla (1937) and others questioned the supposed differences between the two island races. Both were treated as subspecies of the northern Pintail by Delacour (1956) and Johnsgard (1965), but Prevost and Mougin (1970) and Watson (1975) treat them as one species (*A. eatoni*). The Crozet form differs only slightly, with males especially being more buff colored on the chest than in the Kerguelen form. Although Despin et al. (1972) found no significant size differences in their collections from the two archipelagoes, measurements I have taken of specimens from a variety of museums do show small but statistically significant differences for males, with the Crozet form having shorter wings and tail but larger tarsi and culmen. Regardless of whether these minor size and color differences are worthy of taxonomic recognition, data should be recorded separately on these interesting populations.

The recent origin of these forms is inferred from the retention of some seasonal dimorphism in plumages and some vermiculated or finely barred feathers of males. The seasonal differences are much less striking than in northern Pintail males, and the brighter plumage resembles northern males in nonbreeding plumage and seems to be worn during prebreeding. In this plumage males often have a brown head (duller and more streaked than in northern Pintails), occasionally have a light buff line part way around and up the neck, and have grayish vermiculated and brownish-barred side feathers. A small, dull white flank in males may be partially obscured by vermiculations or flecking of black. There are few of the blackish undertail coverts so conspicuous in male northern Pintails. The pure white neck and underside of northern Pintails is replaced by tan feathers delicately streaked with brown, creating a low contrast with the darker dorsal surfaces. Females are darker and more reddish and have only a suggestion of the barred type of plumage common to northern Pintails. The specula of Indian Ocean Pintails are similar in pattern but slightly duller than those of northern Pintails. As in the latter, sexes can be distinguished not only by the conspicuously brighter speculum of the male but by the buff-edged coverts of the wing.

That a dulling of both breeding and eclipse plumages has occurred is apparent from the plain brown feathers of eclipse males. A skin of a flightless Crozet male in the British Museum has only a few vermiculated flank feathers, whereas northern Pintail males in eclipse have considerable vermiculation of their feathers. Unfortunately, this specimen is undated, but Crozet Pintails apparently molt well after the summer breeding period because Goodridge (1839) described chasing flightless ducks for food after a shipwreck during the "cold season." Males in their duller brown plumage can be distinguished from females by plain rather than buff-edged marginal wing coverts and by a brighter speculum. Whereas downy northern Pintails are grayish, Indian Ocean Pintails are brownish, matching the peaty soils of subantarctic islands well. The parental behavior toward young seems not to have been recorded, but Johnsgard (1965) described displays of captive adults.

Numerically, both populations seem secure, but reports are not consistent. Verrill (1895) mentioned an enormous abundance on Kerguelen Island, but Prevost and Mougin (1970) reported them to be relatively more abundant on the Crozets than on Kerguelen. Apparently, these pintails have also been introduced on Amsterdam Island, where they are breeding, and on Saint Paul Island (Prevost and Mougin 1970).

Pacific Island Mallards

The dominant and far-ranging Mallard has given rise to at least three distinct monochromatic insular endemics: the petite Laysan Teal restricted to tiny Laysan Island in the Hawaiian chain; the small, drab

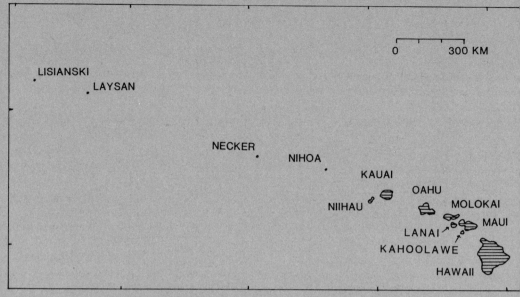

Fig. 1.3. Main Hawaiian Islands.

brown Hawaiian Duck or Koloa originally found on all the larger
Hawaiian Islands; and the Mariana Mallard or Oustelet's Duck (*Anas
platyrhynchos oustaleti*) of the Mariana Islands in the southwest Pacific.
Possibly a fourth form occurred on Lisianski Island in the Hawaiian
chain (see Fig. 1.3) (Clapp and Wirtz 1975). There is little doubt of the
ancestry of these island isolates, but one of these forms may have been an
intermediate ancestor to another.

The Mallard stock could have been of either Asian or North
American origin, but most migrants to the Hawaiian Islands are North
American. All forms originally were named as full species but were
reduced to subspecies of the Mallard by Delacour and Mayr (1945) to
demonstrate ancestral relationships. Ripley (1960) expressed a preference
to treat the Laysan Teal as a full species within the Mallard superspecies.
Brock (1951) listed the Laysan Teal as a subspecies of the Hawaiian Duck
(*A. wyvilliana laysanensis*), a sentiment apparently supported by Warner
(1963) who suggested that the Laysan Teal may have originated from the
Koloa. However, he also referred to the Laysan Teal as a full species (*A.
laysanensis*). Berger (1972) treated both as full species. Since the Koloa
has greater Mallard-like characteristics, it could be that the two forms
evolved from separate waves of pioneers, with the Laysan Teal having
been isolated much earlier. Or periodic invasions of Mallards to Hawaii
may influence the genetic pool of the Koloa. Greenway (1958) suggested
that Pleistocene conditions may have had a profound effect on many

island forms, and it is easy to imagine that movements and pioneering then were drastically different than under present-day conditions.

HAWAIIAN DUCK OR KOLOA. The Hawaiian Duck or Koloa (*Anas platyrhynchos wyvilliana*) is a typical Mallard in shape and action but is smaller, more graceful and less vocal, and lacks the marked sexual dichromatism of the northern Mallard (Fig. 1.4). Nevertheless, sexual dimorphism is sufficiently obvious that sex determination sometimes is possible in the field. Bill color is greenish in males and orange in females, but the color intensity is reduced over that of Mallards. The wing speculum is Mallard-like, but the iridescence tends to be more green than purple, especially in males, and is bordered anteriorly and posteriorly by black. The speculum has a white trailing edge, and occasionally the black stripe has a white anterior. Males in breeding plumage are darker than

Fig. 1.4. Hawaiian Duck or Koloa photographed at the Pohakuloa rearing facility of the Hawaii Division of Fish and Game. This is a male, as indicated by the dark rump, curled central tail feathers, and U-barred body feathers.

females and have a rufous cast to the U-barred chest, green iridescence on the nape, a black rump, and commonly two slightly upturned, black, central tail feathers. The wing coverts of males are plain brown rather than buff edged as in females. Males also have a brown eclipse plumage more similar to that of females (Swedberg 1967). Hens are more buff colored than males but resemble small, dark Mallard hens with reduced color contrast throughout. They lack the prominent barring on body feathers and the curled tail feathers and have less iridescence in the speculum than males. Some individuals of both sexes have white eye-rings.

On Kauai pairs and unpaired birds tend to gather on reservoirs or taro paddies in the evenings, seemingly moving in from isolated territories where they spend the day. In such situations I have observed many of the typical Mallard displays as well as the male's common nod-swimming behavior, as described in captives by Lorenz (1951–53) and Johnsgard (1965). Along lowland streams I saw three-bird chases and other courtship flights that suggest strong territorial or hen defense and show strong powers of flight. Nesting occurs along streams and ditches in sugarcane fields or near reservoirs. Relatively little is known about nesting habits, but the birds are very wary and nest year-round on the ground, with a mean clutch size slightly smaller than that of Mallards. Published data include reports of clutches of 9 and 10 eggs and of 5 nests that had clutches of from 8 to 10 eggs (Munro 1944). Richardson and Bowles (1964) reported clutches of 6, 6, and 8 eggs; one clutch in the wild contained 9 eggs, and clutches of captives were 2, 3, 7, and 7 (Swedberg 1967).

Koloas once occurred on all islands of Hawaii except Lanai and Kahoolawe (Perkins 1903) and used freshwater streams up to 2400 m altitude (Schwartz and Schwartz 1953, Richardson and Bowles 1964); highland forest bogs (Perkins 1903); and, less commonly, coastal lagoons (Munro 1944). Swedberg (1967) estimated that over 90 percent of the Kauai Koloas lived along streams. Hawaiian Ducks feed on freshwater mollusks (Schwartz and Schwartz 1953), insect larvae (Perkins 1903), and earthworms (Munro 1944); but seeds also have been reported as food (Perkins 1903).

Koloas have been much reduced in number and are listed as endangered in the International Council for Bird Protection Red Data Book, vol. 2 (1971). Drainage of wetlands for sugarcane may have been a major factor in their decline (Schwartz and Schwartz 1953). The introduction of the Mongoose (*Herpestes auropuntatus*) also may have influenced their decline; the species survives mainly on Kauai, one of the four islands where mongooses did not occur (Swedberg 1967). Mongooses are favored by sugarcane farmers for rat control, and several specimens have been found on Kauai recently (American Ornithologists'

Union 1978). Other potential predators include rats, cats, dogs, and pigs. Schwartz and Schwartz (1953) estimated that about 500 birds remained in 1953. By intensive surveys devoted only to this species, Swedberg (1967) estimated a total of 3000 birds left on Kauai in the mid-1960s. In spite of their strong flight, no published evidence of interisland movement exists, but it is probable between Kauai and Niihau.

Koloas are being reared at the Pohakuloa facility of the Hawaii Division of Fish and Game on the island of Hawaii. Although they can be reared successfully, the manager of the facility (Ah Fat Lee pers. commun.) says that they never become tame in captivity. Releases of hand-reared birds were made on Kauai in preparation for releases on less intensively used islands (Swedberg 1967), and since then such birds have been released on Oahu and Hawaii. As early as 1903 Perkins noted that variability in plumages might be a product of hybridization with domestic Mallards, but Swedberg (1967) suggested variation was related to age. Such variability may be caused by the presence of an eclipse plumage, by genetic variability of a formerly dichromatic form, or by additional wild pioneers hybridizing with natives. Certainly, great care must be taken in the maintenance of high-quality stock if captives are used for reintroductions.

LAYSAN TEAL. On the basis of wing speculum, feather pattern, bill color, and the males' slightly upturned central tail feathers, the Laysan Teal (*Anas platyrhynchos laysanensis*) is clearly a Mallard derivative (Fig. 1.5). The uncertainty of whether it is an independent Mallard isolate or an offshoot from the Hawaiian Duck has resulted in varying taxonomic treatment. The birds are distinctive by their small size, rufous-tan color, and prominent white eye-rings. According to J. Kear (pers. commun.) they have 9 rather than 10 full-sized primaries plus one tiny marginal primary, but detailed notes taken for me on Laysan by Dr. Daniel Moulton demonstrate that this is variable, with some individuals having 9 and others having 10 full-sized primaries. Some have white throats and extensive white feathering on the head; in captivity, this partial albinism seems to increase (Warner 1963). The female has a pale, dull orange bill with a black saddle, and the male also retains some of the yellowish green and the black saddle of its Mallard ancestor. Males have some iridescent green on the nape. Otherwise the sexes are alike and very dull colored.

Although they can fly, they are more prone to walk or swim and do not seem to leave 500-ha Laysan Island. They are tame and curious (Fisher 1903, Bailey 1956). According to Warner (1963) foods are mostly terrestrial insects (moths) taken at night in territories in which the birds may also nest, but these observations are based on brief field work only. Warner (in Kear 1977) also suggested that a loss of terrestrial insects had

Fig. 1.5. Laysan Teal photographed at Pohakuloa rearing facility of the Hawaii Division of Fish and Game. This is an old male with extensive white on the face, dark body plumage, and slightly upturned central tail feathers.

forced teal to shift to brine shrimp and this had affected their reproductive success. However, such adaptive feeding is common to many island ducks, as will be evident later. This adaptability is reflected in observations reported in Ely and Clapp (1973) and by Eugene Kridler (pers. commun.) that teal regularly feed on brine shrimp and chase shore flies as well.

Whereas downy young of the Koloa are very much like the Mallard in color, the downy Laysan Teal is much darker and more rufous in color and lacks the distinctive eye-stripes and light underparts common to Mallards. Reproductive displays of captives have been described by Johnsgard (1965). Clutch and brood sizes are small, with six eggs or young being the maximum recorded.

Little is known of the species in the wild, in part because it minimizes activity during the heat of the day and seeks shade in the dense vegetation. A long-term study is now under way and should provide insight into how the species survives on this tiny atoll.

The Laysan Teal has the most restricted distribution of any extant duck, living on a rectangular island about 3 km long by 1.5 km wide with a large, central, hypersaline lagoon. The island is a maximum of 12 m above sea level in a zone of severe tropical storms. Teal numbers have fluctuated dramatically, due possibly to plumage hunters who also captured birds for food and to disturbance by airfield construction. But most significant was Rabbit (*Oryctolagus cuniculus*) destruction of habitat between their introduction in 1903 and their extermination in 1923 (Greenway 1958, Warner 1963, Ely and Clapp 1973, Kear 1977). Only 7 birds were seen in 1912–13, but about 700 were estimated in 1961 (Ely and Clapp 1973). Estimates of 500 to 700 birds in the mid-1950s were based on transect samples that were of uncertain accuracy. More recently, Laysan Teal have been surveyed by direct count as they gather to feed on the lagoon in late evening. During the 1970s, counts have been between 214 and 287. However, a study conducted by U.S. Fish and Wildlife Service personnel in 1979 resulted in the banding of about 450 birds and a population estimate nearer 500.

Warner (1963) felt that their survival on Laysan Island has been due to the freshwater pools there and suggested that their loss at Lisianski Island, 185 km west-northwest, may have been due to drying of a freshwater lake. Lisianski Island is a sand and coral mass of only 182 ha. However, Clapp and Wirtz (1975) have suggested that the type of duck found on Lisianski Island was never identified and might have been another endemic form. The presence of several shipwrecked crews there during 1844 to 1846 could have been responsible for the loss of the fairly sizable but very tame population. Moreover, freshwater pools are not always available on Laysan, and the teal use either the lagoon or, less commonly, protected seashore.

While it is true that the Laysan Teal handles easily in captivity and large numbers are in zoos and private collections, the genetic makeup of various flocks is uncertain. Special care must be taken to protect pure stock and preserve the unique feather patterns and island adaptations of this species. Whenever specimens can be obtained, wild-caught teal are used at the Pohakuloa rearing station to maintain the quality of the stock.

MARIANA MALLARD OR OUSTALET'S DUCK. The Mariana Mallard or Oustalet's Duck (*Anas platyrhynchos oustaleti*) is a freshwater form now restricted to small ponds on Saipan in the Mariana Islands (Marshall 1949, Eugene Kridler pers. commun.) and seemingly extirpated from Guam, Rota, and Tinian (Fig. 1.6). Although unlisted in several recent

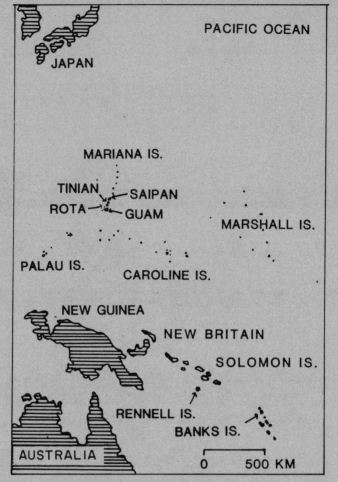

Fig. 1.6. Some major islands of the southwest Pacific Ocean.

taxonomic treatments of waterfowl, this form is of potential importance in understanding duck speciation on islands. The literature is confusing because there are two intergrading plumage forms, one resembling the northern Mallard male in eclipse and another like the New Zealand Gray Duck and Australian Black Duck complex (*A. superciliosa* subspp.) (Yamashina 1948).

Salvadori (1894) originally named this island duck *A. oustaleti* after its collector and suggested that it was related to *A. superciliosa*. Amadon

(1943) and Delacour and Mayr (1945) treated it as a race of the Mallard, being influenced in part by the usual presence of its slightly upturned central pair of tail feathers. On the basis of data from the 50 known skins Yamashina (1948) concluded that the form arose from hybridization of Mallards arriving accidentally in areas inhabited by the Gray Duck (probably the small Palau Islands race, *A. s. pelewensis*). Neither ancestral species presently occurs in the Mariana Islands, but this theory not only explained the dual plumage characters but why the Mallard-type plumage was more common on Saipan while the more abundant *superciliosa* type dominated the southern island of Guam. The six specimens in the American Museum of Natural History are not in full agreement with this pattern, as the two from Saipan are smaller and more like *superciliosa* and the four from Guam are more Mallard-like. These are larger and have a ruddy chest and greener speculum, and two have upturned central tail feathers. However, feather patterns of all show strong affinities to *A. superciliosa*. Because Delacour (1956) considered it a simple hybrid, he dropped it from his list; but both Yamashina (1948) and Amadon (1966) cited the bird as a rare example of natural vertebrate hybridization.

In view of the fact that these islands are closer to the range of Gray Ducks than Mallards and that *A. superciliosa* seems to be a successful species expanding its range (Amadon 1943, Baker 1951), another explanation is possible: Mallard stock in such a remote area possibly was a sedentary isolate like the Hawaiian Duck or Laysan Teal, retaining characters like the curled tail feathers and wing speculum. Swamping may have occurred by populations of Gray Ducks from Palau, 700 km to the southwest. Moreover, since it is now known that Polynesian voyagers were common (Finney 1977), early transport by man cannot be eliminated as a possibility.

Whatever the case, it is still early to abandon this form without further study, and I doubt that Yamashina intended that this be done. In fact, he expressed concerns for its conservation. Greenway (1958) included it in his "Rare and Vanishing Birds" and indicated that it was still present on Saipan, Tinian, and Guam but extinct on Rota. The Mariana Mallard is not found in the International Council for Bird Protection Red Data Book (1971) of endangered species, presumably because of its absence from recent taxonomic revisions. However, a recent list of endangered species used by the U.S. Fish and Wildlife Service in regulating international trade (Federal Register, 22 February 1977) now includes the form. Eugene Kridler (pers. commun.) reported seeing two of the birds on Saipan in 1978 and captured a male in February and a female in May of 1979. He estimates that less than 25 are left in the wild, making it the rarest of all endemic island forms. Regardless of its origins, the bird must be protected fully and studied further (Ripley 1957).

Rennell Gray Teal, Andaman Teal, and Madagascar Teal

The Gray Teal (*Anas gibberifrons*) is widespread in the Australasian Region, and variation is strongly influenced by isolation on islands. Moreover, their irregular distribution suggests great variation in suitable habitat on these tropical islands. Delacour (1956) accepted four subspecies: *gracilis* in Australia, New Guinea, and New Zealand; *remissa* on Rennell Island in the Solomons (Fig. 1.6); *gibberifrons* in the East Indies (Java, Celebes, and smaller nearby islands); and *albogularis* on the Andaman Islands in the Bay of Bengal.

The smallest race of the Gray Teal (*remissa*) was found only on Rennell Island and is characterized by a low forehead, petite bill, and darker coloration. It is perhaps more buff than rufous on the underparts compared to the equally dark *gibberifrons*. Nothing is known of the biology of this form, but it lives on an atoll (68 km by 19 km) with a large lake (16 km by 5 km) (Lake Te-nggano; see Wolff 1958) isolated by 170 km from San Cristobal and 200 km from Guadalcanal. Yet the Gray Teal was only recorded once in the Solomons (Mayr 1931). Kear and Williams (1978) report that this teal is now extinct, possibly because of competition with fish (*Tilapia* sp.) introduced into the lake.

The only form sufficiently unique that it often was regarded as a full species is the Andaman Teal or Oceanic Teal (referred to as *A. albogularis*). Originally placed in the genus *Mareca* by Hume (1873), presumably because of its wigeonlike wing, Baker (1899) referred to it as *Nettion,* an early generic name for teal. Phillips (1923) later placed it in the genus *Anas* as a full species.

The Andaman Teal is a dark grayish brown with a dark brown crown and back, a distinctive white eye-ring, and sometimes a white face. Like the Laysan Teal (Warner 1963) adults show varying degrees of albinism on the head and neck, which increases in captivity (Delacour 1956). Wright and Dewar (1925) discussed this coloration in Andaman Teal and suggested that the bird's isolation on the Andaman Islands induced such plumage changes. Moreover, they predicted that eventually the species would be fully white headed.

Relatively little is known of the biology of the Andaman Teal, but they live in tropical forests and perch readily, often using mangroves as roost sites. During nonbreeding periods, they feed mostly at night in saline lagoons and rice paddies. The Andaman Teal prefers forest streams for nesting (Hume and Marshall 1880), but the nest site is uncertain. Osmaston (1906) reported 10 eggs in a tree hole in August; another report is of 1 egg on the ground. Nesting seems to occur during July to August (Butler 1896) and parental care involves both sexes (Baker 1899). Ali and Ripley (1968) suggested that while plant foods dominate, the birds probably eat insects, worms, and crustaceans as well.

Another closely related duck is the indigenous Madagascar or Bernier's Teal (*A. bernieri*). Delacour (1956) considered it an erythristic form of the Gray Teal, but he retained it as a full species, in part because of its isolation but also for lack of data. It is said to be rare, and Ripley (1942) was unable to examine skeletal material in his review of the group. More recently, Scott and Lubbock (1974) reported about 120 at Lake Bemamba in western Madagascar. It is isolated from any other member of the group; although it has a similar wing speculum, it has a brown rather than red iris and orange or light red rather than gray bill and feet. It lacks the definite spotting on the breast, and the throat is tan flecked with brown rather than white as in the Gray Teal. Although often pictured as uniform in color, the back is considerably darker than the underparts. This bird lacks the distinctly dark crown of the Gray Teal. Its nest and eggs are unknown, but it reportedly nests in the southern summer, November to April.

Ripley (1942) and others have drawn attention to certain similarities of the Gray Teal and the Chestnut Teal (*A. castanea*) of Australia, but while Gray Teal are sexually monochromatic, the Chestnut Teal is strongly dichromatic. The male has a green head; bright chestnut chest, side, and belly; white flank; and black tail area. Female Chestnut Teal and Gray Teal are so similar that the two species are difficult to distinguish (Ripley 1942, Frith 1967), and I suspect that much museum material is incorrectly labeled. Both the Gray Teal and the Chestnut Teal have red irises and wigeonlike specula. Ripley (1942) considered the two conspecific, but Delacour (1956) treated them as species because they breed sympatrically. It is possible that the Chestnut Teal evolved as a high-latitude, dichromatic form that had its origin from a more tropical and insular monochromatic Gray Teal, as may have occurred in the origin of northern species of the genus *Anas*.

South Georgia Pintail

The South Georgia Pintail (*Anas georgica georgica*) (Fig. 1.7) is a diminutive form of the monochromatic South American Brown or Yellow-billed Pintail (*A. g. spinicauda*) that lives on the archipelago of South Georgia at lat. 55° S (Fig. 1.8). These islands are about 1500 km east of the closest source of ancestral stock, the Falkland Islands, where the Yellow-billed Pintail occurs but is not abundant (Cawkell and Hamilton 1961, Weller 1972).

Few other ducks rival the continental form of the Brown Pintail in being a drab and uniform brown. The head is tan flecked with dark brown, whereas feathers on the remainder of the body are dark and centrally edged with buff. The upperparts are darker than the ventral area,

Fig. 1.7. A pair of South Georgia Pintails on boulder shoreline with King Penguins (*Aptenodytes patagonicus*) and Elephant Seals (*Mirounga leonina*).

and the belly may be whitish. Compared to the continental race, the island form is much smaller in body size and extremities (Delacour 1956, Lack 1970), is darker in color, and has a shorter and duller bill. The wing speculum is virtually the same as that of the Brown Pintail but is slightly duller. Although superficially monomorphic, males can be distinguished by longer and blacker tertials, darker and more iridescent specula, and the absence of buff edges on the marginal coverts of the wing. Murphy (1916) noted that the South Georgia bird has 16 rather than 14 tail feathers. Although this tendency does exist, many Brown Pintails also have 16 tail feathers, and a few South Georgia Pintails even have 18.

Because of its petite features and small size, this form has for many years been termed South Georgia Teal, and has even been referred to by generic terms used for teal (*Nettion, Nettium,* or *Querquedula*). Murphy (1916) first demonstrated that it was merely an insular form of the Brown Pintail. He retained the bird as a full species because of its isolation; Delacour and Mayr (1945) relegated it to subspecific rank to show its close relationship to the continental form. The island form, named first, became the nominate form of the species that occurs throughout much of temperate South America.

Although there has been little change in feather color or pattern due to isolation, the ancestral Brown Pintail is a drab bird that already lacks the vermiculations or distinctive barring common to northern Pintails. In addition, invasions of ancestral stock may still be occurring. The Speckled Teal (*Anas flavirostris*) has become established as a breeding bird on South Georgia (Weller and Howard 1972), but the Speckled Teal and the Brown Pintail are sympatric over much of their continental range and do not hybridize (Johnsgard 1965).

Presumably never numerous and ecologically restricted in distribution to freshwater basins near the sea, the South Georgia Pintail population probably exceeds 2000 and is as abundant as can be expected for the available habitat. Hunting pressure once exerted by sealers and whalers (Murphy 1916) has been ended by the virtual absence of these activities in the southern oceans at the present time, and there are no permanent human residents on the island.

The breeding behavior of the species has been described by Murphy (1916) and Weller (1975c) and resembles that of all pintails. Clutches are small, and the downy young may be accompanied by one or both

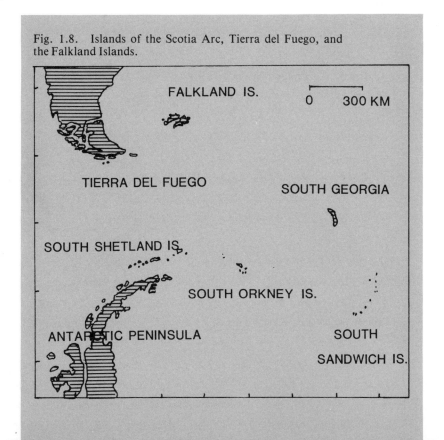

Fig. 1.8. Islands of the Scotia Arc, Tierra del Fuego, and the Falkland Islands.

FALKLAND IS.

0   300 KM

TIERRA DEL FUEGO

SOUTH GEORGIA

SOUTH SHETLAND IS.

SOUTH ORKNEY IS.

ANTARCTIC PENINSULA

SOUTH

SANDWICH IS.

parents. The downies are the darkest and brownest of all pintails, even having a dark cast to the underparts.

Meller's Duck

The large, dark, rufous brown, Mallard-like Meller's Duck (*Anas melleri*) is endemic in eastern Madagascar and seems to have been introduced in Mauritius, 840 km to the east. It is generally mottled dark brown above and lighter brown below with a flecked head that has a darker crown. It is lighter and less uniform in color than the North American Black Duck (*A. rubripes*). The wing speculum is a brilliant emerald, but with some purple sheen. Both sexes are similar, but the bill of the male is longer and the speculum is more brilliant and generally has less white and buff edging. Its displays are Mallard-like except that males are extremely aggressive and have an independent nod-swimming display like female Mallards (Lorenz 1951–53). This is also typical of the Hawaiian Duck and the Laysan Teal (Johnsgard 1965). Based on observation of captives, Lorenz (1951–53) indicated that the bills of both sexes were the same color; descriptions of soft parts on specimen labels indicate orange feet and an olive green bill with a black nail. Johnsgard (1965) considered the bird no more different from a Mallard than the Black Duck; and it may well represent a fairly recent, southern hemisphere isolate of the Eurasian Mallard (or the primitive stock from which northern Mallards evolved). Like several other southern *Anas* species that lack clear-cut sexual dimorphism, the wing coverts are buff edged in both sexes. Whether plumages differ by season is uncertain.

The species seems to be uncommon. There are no recent observations on Madagascar; Todd (1979) reported only 20 pairs remaining on Mauritius in 1977.

Madagascar White-eye and Other White-eyes

The White-eyes (*Aythya* spp.) are a widespread group of freshwater diving ducks that occur in Eurasia, New Guinea, and Australia. Although commonly considered monochromatic, all species of White-eyes have sexual dichromatism in plumage color, but it simply is not as dramatic as in most northern hemisphere ducks. The male Baer's White-eye (*A. baeri*), with its iridescent green head and ferruginous chest, is the most distinctive from the brown female. The male of the Eurasian Common White-eye or Ferruginous Duck (*A. nyroca*) has a ferruginous head as well as chest, also differing distinctively from the brown female. The sexes are most similar in the Australian White-eye (*A. australis*), but the male's darker head and chest color are still apparent.

The Australian White-eye is widely distributed on islands mostly to the northeast of Australia, and several forms seem to be racially distinct. Only the population living on the Banks Islands, north of the New Hebrides in the Coral Sea, has been treated as a separate subspecies (*A. australis exima*), but the New Guinea population also seems to be distinctive in color (Delacour 1964).

The Madagascar White-eye (*A. innotata*) is distinctively dichromatic, and the male is more like a Baer's White-eye in color than like a Common White-eye. The male's chest is a very dark rufous brown, and the head and neck are dark brown or black with some greenish iridescence on the nape, and the head has a rufous crown. However, the bill morphology of the Madagascar form is more like the Common White-eye than the Baer's White-eye. The white belly contrasts with the brown back, side, and tail. The female is brown with whitish underparts. Both have white throughout the secondaries and primaries of the otherwise dark brown wing, but it is brighter in the male. The undertail coverts are white as in other white-eyes. The presence of an eclipse plumage in males is uncertain.

According to Delacour (1959) this species is common only on the large highland lakes such as Alaotra of eastern Madagascar at an altitude of 1000 m or more. He finds that the species is more like a Redhead (*A. americana*) in head and body shape than like the Common White-eye from which one might logically assume (from their respective ranges) that it originated (Johnsgard 1965). The species seems to be a typical diving duck, feeding by diving in freshwater lakes. Otherwise, nothing is known of its breeding biology or ecology.

Steamer Ducks

Few ducks have caused more taxonomic confusion than have steamer ducks (*Tachyeres* spp.) which are massive diving ducks that reside at the tip of South America and on Tierra del Fuego and the Falkland Islands (Fig. 1.8). Many pages have been written about whether they could or would not fly and on the number of species in existence. Murphy (1936) resolved the issue by declaring one flying and two flightless species, the former sympatric with two allopatric flightless forms of the Falkland Islands and the Magellanic region. But the issue of a flying and flightless form in the Magellanic region had clearly been resolved by several field ornithologists earlier (Blaauw 1916, Lowe 1934); their findings simply were not accepted.

All steamer ducks are large by duck standards, weighing from about

Fig. 1.9.   A pair of nonbreeding Falkland Flightless Steamer Ducks.

2200 g to 6300 g. They are gray with white patches in the speculum and a stout bill. The Flying Steamer Duck (*T. patachonicus*) is the smallest of the three; males weigh up to 3200 g, but they still take flight with difficulty. These ducks seem to be the least common of the three, but because they can fly, they are more widespread, occurring throughout Patagonia, Tierra del Fuego, and the Falkland Islands. The two currently accepted flightless species (*T. pteneres* of the Magellanic region (Fig. 1.9) and *T. brachypterus* of the Falklands) differ in size with up to 4000 g for male *brachypterus* and up to 6300 g for male *pteneres*. They also differ in color in that the Falkland form is more sexually dichromatic, with the male's head being whitish. Additionally, the body color is characteristically wine and gray rather than gray, and the ducklings differ in color pattern (Weller 1976). Both flightless species are abundant along coastlines.

They are skilled divers and favor open water (Humphrey et al. 1970, Weller 1972). The flying species uses freshwater lakes, estuaries, or protected marine channels, whereas the flightless forms may be found on more open and rugged marine coastlines (Weller 1976). No behavioral or ecological differences have been recorded, but all three species need serious study. Murphy (1936) retained two full species of Flightless Steamer Ducks because of the similarity of the flying and flightless forms in the Falkland Islands. However, this treatment is inconsistent with current treatment of the Brown Teal and other ducks.

Although data are not as clear-cut for the flying form, the two flightless forms defend territories actively, and violent battles are common. Males remain on territory while the female incubates, and they assist in care of the brood. At maturation the young are chased from the territory and gather and remain in large flocks, possibly until they are several years of age (Weller 1976).

The flightless marine species feeds on large, benthic invertebrates; the flying species feeds on clams and snails of freshwater lakes, but the foods in coastal areas are unknown. Populations of all three seem secure.

Brown Teal and Flightless Teal

The Brown Teal (*Anas aucklandica chlorotis*) of New Zealand is itself a typical island duck, being small and dark with minimal dichromatism. Its brightest plumage is remarkably similar in general color pattern to that of the Chestnut Teal of Australia from which many think it is derived. However, Ripley (1942) considered the Chestnut Teal as the nominate form of the Gray Teal. Eyton (1838) originally placed the Chestnut Teal in the genus *Mareca,* once used for all wigeons. Scott (1958), however, pointed out that whereas the Chestnut Teal has a wigeonlike speculum of white, black, and green, the speculum of the Brown Teal is pintail-like, being buff-edged, iridescent black. Further, Johnsgard (1965) noted the absence of vermiculations in the Chestnut Teal that are common to both the Brown Teal and the Auckland Flightless Teal (*A. a. aucklandica*). Possibly these plumage differences represent minor genetic changes, but it seems best to treat Chestnut, Gray, and Brown teal as separate species as suggested by Delacour (1956), while recognizing the need for serious study of this complex. I will consider here only the New Zealand Brown Teal and its presumed derivative, the Flightless Teal (Salvadori 1895, Newton 1896, Delacour 1956).

The Brown Teal demonstrates considerable variation in plumage, with minimal sexual dimorphism and subdued patterns. In males the generally plain brown head and neck have a greenish sheen that is especially prominent in the breeding plumage. A few males have a bronze sheen on the crown, green iridescence below, and a black nape reminis-

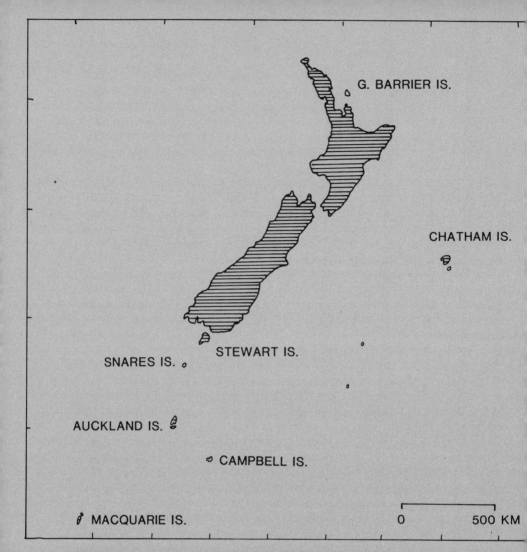

Fig. 1.10.   Important islands surrounding New Zealand.

cent of the Falcated Teal (*A. falcata*). A light tan to white neck band is present on brighter males and separates the dark head from the reddish chest. These patterns are similar to the Chestnut Teal, but color contrast is much subdued. The lower belly, typically pale chestnut spotted with black in the Chestnut Teal, is dull tan that is weakly spotted or barred with darker brown. Vermiculated flank, side, or back feathers are not uncommon in the brightest plumage. The undertail coverts are black, a white spot flecked with black on the side of the tail may be present, and black tertials are not uncommon.

Some males are a plain, femalelike brown with little or no pattern. Flocks of birds seen in the postbreeding period (Weller 1974) lacked greenish iridescence on the head or any of the more colorful patterns of certain males. Thus it appears that an eclipse or nonbreeding plumage is retained despite the dullness of the breeding plumage. In this regard, the species resembles most of the quasi-dimorphic isolates mentioned previously.

Females are plain brown, lacking barring or vermiculations, but have buff edging to their brown feathers. This is true also of the marginal wing coverts, so that even flightless males in eclipse may be recognized by their plain-colored wing coverts. Males also have more colorful wing specula.

The Brown Teal is one of the rarest of all ducks, now residing only in small and isolated populations on both main islands of New Zealand but being most abundant on Great Barrier Island (Weller 1974) (Fig. 1.10). It is a highly terrestrial duck but also feeds in the shallows of estuaries. Little is known of its breeding biology and nesting ecology.

The Auckland Flightless Teal was named *Nesonetta aucklandica* by Gray (1844), and it has become the nominate form in current taxonomic treatment of the New Zealand Brown Teal complex (Delacour 1956, Johnsgard 1965). The discovery of a similar teal on the Campbell Islands (275 km to the southeast) induced Fleming (1935) to erect a new genus (*Xenonetta nesiotis*), which was not accepted, and *nesiotis* now is regarded as the Campbell Island subspecies. Only two specimens of the Campbell Flightless Teal have been collected, and the race was thought extinct until a recent expedition of the New Zealand Wildlife Service captured one individual on the minute Dent Island in the Campbells in November 1975. Others were seen, and a population of 30 to 50 birds was estimated (Robertson 1976). Certainly, there has been little possibility of exchange between the two populations, but the duration of the isolation on the Campbell Islands is uncertain.

The Auckland Flightless Teal is less variable in color than the Brown Teal, and differences between breeding and eclipse plumages are less marked (Falla and Stead 1938). The male in breeding plumage has a brown head with green iridescence on the nape; the chest is slightly more rufous than the remaining reddish brown plumage of the body; and extensive brownish vermiculations are present on the sides, scapulars, and flank. The flank is not as white as in the Brown and Chestnut teal, and there is no white neck band. A white eye-ring surrounds the brown iris. The chest is lightly spotted, and the belly is somewhat dusky and barred, rather than spotted as in the Brown Teal. Males in the duller, presumably nonbreeding, plumage have reduced vermiculations. Females lack vermiculations or other patterning in their reddish brown feathers. The throat often is flecked with white (Falla and Stead 1938), and the lower belly may be a dull white. Both sexes lack a speculum but have a narrow white trailing edge to the secondaries of their very abbreviated wings. Males may have some iridescence in the wing, but both sexes have a deep green iridescence on the back—a feature less conspicuous in the Brown Teal. Gadow (1902) found a reduction in the number of primaries from the normal 11 (eleventh much reduced) to 10 (tenth much reduced) or even 9. In the specimens I have checked, both sexes had 10 primaries—9 large plus 1 reduced. Although the Flightless Teal strongly resembles the Brown Teal, its lack of distinctive color patterns masks the years of evolutionary pressures that have produced a drab, flightless terrestrial duck uniquely adapted to these rugged islands.

The status of the Auckland Flightless Teal is difficult to assess because they are scattered in small numbers on all the islets surrounding the main Auckland Island. Certainly hundreds exist, and their numbers possibly exceed 1000. Their absence on the main island is attributed to introduced cats and pigs, and the safety of the species is dependent on prevention of the spread of these potential predators to the smaller

Fig. 1.11.   Male Auckland Island Flightless Teal feeding on invertebrates in decaying, wind-rowed kelp along Ewing Island, Auckland group.

Fig. 1.12. Solitary Auckland Island Flightless Teal in a small *Carex*-rimmed pool along the shore of Ewing Island, Auckland group.

islands. Most populations of this highly terrestrial duck are dependent on the sea or seashore where they feed by a variety of methods, but they use the rare freshwater pools as well (Weller 1975d) (Figs. 1.11, and 1.12). Their courtship occurs on or near water and involves aggressive chases and escape diving. Only a few nests of very small clutches have been found, and the rearing behavior is unknown.

New Zealand Shelduck or Paradise Duck

The gaudy New Zealand Shelduck or Paradise Duck (*Tadorna variegata*) is much like the Australian Shelduck (*T. tadornoides*) in color. Johnsgard (1965) and J. Kear (pers. commun.) have noted similarities to the African or Cape Shelduck (*T. cana*). Whereas male and female Australian Shelducks differ only in a white eye-patch on the female (and sometimes more white elsewhere on the face or body) and a slightly wider white neck band in the male, the female New Zealand Shelduck is white headed with an almost totally rufous body. The male is black headed like the Australian form but has little rufous color on the body; it is nearly totally black on the head, chest, back of the neck, and rump where the female is rufous and is vermiculated black on dull white on the back, sides, and underparts. Although both sexes have two molts per year, the female loses the rufous color during the nonbreeding period. Distinctive sexual dichromatism is characteristic of several New Zealand anatids, but such seasonal dichromatism is rare in southern anatids.

On both the North and South islands of New Zealand, Paradise Ducks occur as territorial pairs along mountain streams, where they graze on upland grasses, sedges, and some aquatic plants (Bisset 1976). They may also take invertebrates, possibly incidental to other foods, but this is still uncertain. Some shelducks are seen in estuaries, but their foods there are unknown. Fitzgerald (1969) noted that they molt on large lakes near Rotorua on North Island and that females disperse in spring with several males, finally eliminating all but one. Bisset (1976), however, suggests that pairs rarely leave their territories in grassy areas along South Island streams; my limited observations along rapid streams on North Island are in agreement. Flocks of nonbreeders (possibly up to 18 months of age) frequent large and often cultivated clover fields (Bisset 1976, McAllum 1965).

Paradise Ducks nest in dense vegetation and crevices or in holes up to 6 m above the ground (Delacour 1954, Falla et al. 1967).

Philippine Duck

The Philippine Duck (*Anas luzonica*) is a distinctively colored, sexually monomorphic, tropical species endemic in the Philippines. Its origins undoubtedly are from the Mallard-like Chinese Spotbill (*A. poecilorhyncha*) or the Australian–New Zealand *A. superciliosa* complex. It is, however, a very distinct form that lacks the spots, streaks, or mottling of those possible ancestors. The body is uniformly gray brown, being darkest on the back and lightest on the chest. The head and neck are a contrasting rufous color highlighted by a dark crown and eye-stripe. The wing speculum is bright green with some purple iridescence, bordered prominently by black and a little white. The hen is slightly smaller than the drake.

The displays of the Philippine Duck are Mallard-like, but with an exaggerated nod-swimming by the male. Jones (1953) and Jones in

Delacour (1956) described the Mallard-like behavior but noted no interest of a male Philippine Duck in female Mallards. However, hybrids between the Philippine Duck and the Gray Duck are known in captivity (Johnsgard 1960).

Little is known of its life history or ecology. The endemic Philippine Duck is an inland, freshwater species that occurs at low altitudes and frequents marshes. Apparently it is widespread but is not common anywhere. It uses rivers in some areas (McGregor 1905) but not in others (Rand and Rabor 1960) and prefers small ponds to large lakes (Ripley and Rabor 1958).

Island Whistling Ducks

The genus *Dendrocygna* is a widespread group with several forms strongly influenced by isolation on islands. In most cases, these are not restricted to single islands or even small or isolated archipelagoes, but their insular population characteristics are nonetheless apparent. Island derivatives of one species differ only subspecifically; two are distinct species.

The Wandering Whistling Duck (*D. arcuata*) has three races differentiated only in size: The East Indian form (*D. a. arcuata*) is intermediate in size and found only in the East Indies, including Borneo, Sumatra, Celebes, Moluccas, and Philippines. The smallest race, the Lesser Wandering Whistling Duck (*D. a. pygmaea*) is restricted to New Britain, but it formerly occurred on the Fiji Islands until eliminated by the introduced mongoose (Delacour 1954). The Australia Wandering Whistling Duck (*D. a. australis*) is the largest and is found in New Guinea and Australia. All races apparently nest on the ground (Frith 1967, Rand and Gilliard 1967).

The two distinctive island species are strikingly similar in color and nest in tree holes, but they are widely separated geographically: the Spotted Whistling Duck (*D. guttata*) is an abundant species that overlaps with *D. a. arcuata* in the East Indies; the Cuban or Black-billed Whistling Duck (*D. arborea*) occurs sparingly in the West Indies (Bahama, Cuba, Haiti, Jamaica, Puerto Rico, Virgin Islands, and Martinique), where it has suffered losses due to the introduced mongoose (Kear and Williams 1978) and habitat destruction. Although considerably smaller, *D. guttata* is difficult to separate from *D. arborea* following most published descriptions. Both have a dark brown crown and dorsal neck; tan face; brown-flecked neck; rusty, spotty cheek; light tan underparts that are spotted brown; dark brown back with rufous-edged feathers; and bold, cream-colored spots on dark brown side and flank feathers. The most distinctive features are the black rather than reddish bill, the cinnamon color above the eye, and the broader mandibular nail of *D. arborea*. Also, *D. arborea* has creamy white chest spots with a broad dark brown distal band, whereas such spots on *D. guttata* have more brown proximate to the cream spots than distal to them. The cream-colored spots of the side and flank are more rounded and have much less dark crossbarring on *D. guttata*.

Auckland Merganser

The Auckland Merganser (*Mergus australis*), seemingly now extinct, was one of only two southern hemisphere mergansers. It is known from only casual observations by seamen and naturalists and from 26 specimens taken from 1840 to 1902 (Kear and Scarlett 1970). Fossil evidence indicated that it once occurred at least on South Island of New Zealand and that the Auckland population represented the last remnant of the species (see Fig. 1.10). Whereas typical northern hemisphere mergansers are strongly dichromatic and most males have green heads and females have brown heads, the southern species are monomorphic and both sexes are either green (Brazilian Merganser, *M. octosetaceus*) or rufous brown (Auckland Merganser). Based on culmen of the specimens, males were larger than females, and they probably had more white in the wing. However, the white is much reduced compared to northern species. Although the wings seem small, the merganser was capable of flight. A reduced crest seems more prominent in males. Dr. Kenneth Parkes has pointed out to me that the tail is short and not stiff like those of other mergansers. The upperparts are dark and rather rufous brown; the chest is grayish brown with a gradual transition into the rufous neck and head, and the belly is off-white and often mottled with a gray brown. The bill and feet probably were orange, as they still show this color in the skins. The downy duckling is a beautiful rich brown with a more cinnamon head and lighter cinnamon throat; the belly is a contrasting drab white.

Although the Auckland form resembles the Red-breasted Merganser (*M. serrator*) in size, its bill morphology is more nearly that of the Common Merganser (*M. merganser*) or the Chinese Merganser (*M. squamatus*). The nail of the bill is more like that of the Chinese Merganser. The same similarity exists in the osseus bulla (Humphrey 1955).

Kear and Scarlett (1970) summarized what is known of the biology of the species. Casual reports suggest that the species frequented the deep pools of larger streams and probably fed in brackish estuaries. The few foods taken from stomachs include the freshwater stream fish *Galaxias brevipennis* and a few marine invertebrates—a polychaete and a cephalopod. Nest sites and egg and clutch sizes are unknown, but four, dark-colored, downy ducklings were collected—probably from the same brood. Although the streams are still present and *Galaxias* is still abundant, the main island of the Aucklands has been inhabited by wild pigs, feral domestic cats, and other exotic predators, so that nests over a large portion of the range must have been subjected to a new pressure. Adams Island, the southernmost island of the Auckland archipelago, has never had rats, cats, or pigs, but its streams and estuaries are small and probably never held a large population (Williams and Weller 1974).

New Zealand Scaup

The New Zealand Scaup (*Aythya novae-seelandiae*) is a remote isolate of either the strongly migratory and wide-ranging Lesser Scaup (*A. affinis*)–Greater Scaup (*A. marila*) complex of the northern hemisphere or possibly the northern Tufted Duck (*A. fulvigula*). There is marked sexual dichromatism but seemingly no seasonal dichromatism. Known in New Zealand as the Black Teal, the male is the darkest of all diving ducks, rivaled only by the scoters (*Melanitta* spp.) in color. The male is generally brownish black with an iridescent green on the black head and occasionally on the back, and the eye is yellow. The female is a uniform brown, with a more rufous side and whitish underparts and a brown eye. There may be white surrounding the base of the bill in some plumages, as is true of northern scaup during the spring courtship period. As in other scaup an indefinite, linear white area is present in the wing and is most prominent in the secondaries.

This bird is common on a few of the larger lakes of New Zealand; general observations on its biology have been reported by Oliver (1955) and Delacour (1959). It is highly social in the nonbreeding periods, and flocks seen during the breeding period (October through March) imply that they do not mature until two years of age (Falla et al. 1967). Flocks frequent large, shallow, freshwater lakes on both North Island and South Island of New Zealand. The bird feeds by diving in dense submergent vegetation in 1.5 m to 2 m of water, but its foods are unknown. It nests in tall vegetation along the shore and flies very little unless disturbed. Reid and Roderick (1973) have successfully reared significant numbers for possible release in new areas.

Salvadori's Duck

The general impression of Salvadori's Duck (*Anas* [= *Salvadorina*] *waiguiensis*) is a bird with a blackish brown head, a relatively short yellow bill, and dark blackish brown upperparts crossed by conspicuous white crossbars. The long tail is typical of stream specialists and is plain colored in most specimens, but young birds especially have barred tails. The overlapping upper tail coverts also are barred. The light cream chest has dark spotting, and the more grayish undertail area is more heavily but less distinctly spotted. Prominent white bars cross the dark side feathers. Sexual dichromatism is not evident, but the female is smaller.

This fascinating little duck occurs in high, mountain stream pools and in lakes from 450 m to 4000 m altitude in New Guinea. It was extensively collected during several major expeditions, but little is known of its life history. Rand and Gilliard (1967), Kear (1975), and Diamond (1972) have summarized its distribution and general habitat preferences, but few comments have been made on behavior or breeding biology. Its taxonomic status is an enigma, for although it has an *Anas*-like speculum, its body form more nearly resembles a Blue Mountain Duck (*Hymenolaimus malacorhynchos*) or a Torrent Duck (*Merganetta armata*) with its elongate body and tail. Johnsgard (1965) pointed out several similarities of this species with torrent ducks but also cited some *Anas*-like displays. According to Kear (1975) it is territorial and only seen in pairs. The birds regularly dive for food in these mountain streams probably for stream insects. This species needs detailed study of courtship, breeding biology, and habitat selection.

Hawaiian Goose or Nene

One of the most terrestrial of all waterfowl, the Hawaiian Goose or Nene (*Branta sandvicensis*) is a unique island species that is one of few extant island waterfowl and the only island goose to reach species level if not generic level of differentiation (Fig. 1.13). It lives on the dry, highland slopes of Mauna Loa at altitudes of 1500 m to 2200 m on the island of Hawaii and now by reintroduction on the island of Maui. Prior to 1900 it probably occurred near sea level on Hawaii (Baldwin 1945). Presumably it is an island isolate of stock similar to the Canada Goose (*B. canadensis*) that still reaches the islands, but its color is tan and barred, the webbing of the feet is reduced, the neck contains "furrowing" common to some species of the genus *Anser,* and the facial and neck color patterns are unique.

In size the Hawaiian Goose is closest to the Cackling Canada Goose (*B. c. minima*) or the Aleutian Canada Goose (*B. c. leucopareia*), possible ancestors. Weights of captive birds were provided by Ah Fat Lee of the Hawaii Division of Fish and Game: 27 prenesting females weighed 1930 g (± S. D. 166 g) and 29 postmolt females weighed 1795g (± S.D. 143 g). Males were slightly heavier: 2010g (± S.D. 152 g) and 1928g (± S.D. 388 g) respectively.

Fig. 1.13. Hawaiian Goose or Nene photographed at the Pohakuloa rearing station of the Hawaii Division of Fish and Game, showing prominent neck furrows and reduced webbing between the toes.

On Hawaii the geese breed in very dry sites that may lack standing water but where berry-producing shrubs and forage grasses are abundant. Conditions are drastically different on Maui where the rainfall exceeds 600 cm per year, and Kear and Williams (1978) suggest that this population fared well during the severe drought on that island. Nests are most common in winter sheltered spots where clutches of 5 to 8 are deposited. Little is known of natural foods, nesting, and general behavior of the wild birds.

Once regarded as the most endangered of waterfowl, the species has been bred successfully by numerous individuals; the Hawaii Division of Fish and Game and the Wildfowl Trust have released some 1600 birds since 1962. According to Baldwin (1945) less than 50 were left in the 1940s, only on the Island of Hawaii, of a population that must have numbered in the thousands in the eighteenth century. Estimates in 1975 were 600 birds on Hawaii and 100 on Maui (American Ornithologists' Union 1975). Lubbock (1975) reported on the success of introduced geese observed in the Haleakala Crater on Maui, where he saw 60 geese and resident workers estimated that many more birds lived. Pigs and mongooses apparently occur in the area but are controlled. Goats also may compete for foods, and fencing and goat control are being considered for several national parks. Releases are now being minimized, and an evaluation of past releases is being made by the Hawaii Division of Fish and Game. An additional approach to establishment is the slow-release method being employed by Paul Banko of the National Park Service. He is using large pens at several altitudes and in different vegetative types. Free-flying wild birds can enter the pens, and young can leave at will. It is hoped the species will be able to maintain itself under these various management and protection programs.

Blue Mountain Duck

The Blue Mountain Duck (*Hymenolaimus malacorhynchos*) is a unique, endemic monotypic genus that is a classic island isolate, without any known close relatives. It frequents pools and riffles on fast mountain streams, where pairs aggressively maintain territories in which they feed on caddis flies (Kear and Steel 1971) and dipterans (Craig 1974). They nest in October and November in holes and crevices and lay small clutches as do other island stream ducks. The species range throughout appropriate mountain streams in New Zealand.

The sexes are alike in plumage, but females are slightly smaller (Delacour 1956). The head and body are a uniform gray, with light brownish spotting on the upper back and burnt orange or chestnut spotting on the breast. Full-grown but immature birds are similar in plumage but have less definite patterns and duller feathers. The wing is generally plain, but there is a trailing edge of white on the secondaries and some of the same on a lateral edging of black on the tertials. Variation in the white edging should be investigated as a criterion of age or sex. The iris is yellow, the yellow bill has flexible and membranous flaps hanging down from either edge of the upper mandible, and the legs are brown. The downy young have a unique vertical bar above the eye-stripe (Kear 1973), which is also found in the Torrent Duck and the Black-headed Duck (*Heteronetta atricapilla*) (Weller 1968b).

Despite considerable past and current study, much is yet to be learned about this species in relation to pair bonds, territoriality, foods, and brood-rearing behavior.

Factors Influencing Colonization

Characteristics of Pioneering Island Anatids

IN SPITE of the speculative nature of assessing characteristics of past pioneers on the basis of presumed present-day ancestors, it is worth searching for patterns. Lack (1970) pointed out that most island endemics are representatives of the dabbling duck (genus *Anas*), the most widespread and adaptable group of ducks. In connection with repopulation of continental areas Hochbaum (1946) cited many of the characters that make this genus a pioneering group: mobility, terrestrial nesting, adaptability in foods, preference for small and even temporary wetlands, and a high reproductive rate based strongly on renesting potential. Most are also breeding birds of unstable habitats, where seasonal migration has resulted in adaptations to various wetland types and food resources (Weller 1975e). Flocking at feeding areas is common, especially in winter, and many of the birds have bills adapted to a variety of food sizes and types.

Several of the group have populations or ancestors that seasonally or regularly use estuaries or saline lagoons and thus are preadapted to the versatility essential for survival on oceanic islands. The Brown Teal of New Zealand, essentially an island isolate in color and behavior, feeds on land and in estuaries. Its possible ancestor, the Chestnut Teal, is essentially an estuarine bird (Frith 1967). The Australasian Gray Duck and Black Duck complex is an expanding island pioneer that seems able to use a variety of wetland types. Many of the isolates originated from migratory Mallards, Pintails, and Gadwalls, all of which use alkaline waters during breeding and often use brackish waters in winter. In addition to using estuaries, the Brown Pintail breeds on alkaline lakes in both the high Andes and the pampas of Argentina (Weller 1968a).

Although we commonly speak of ducks as freshwater birds, a few species are strictly marine (eiders and steamer ducks), and species of several genera winter in saline water. Thus it is not surprising that water-fowl have well-developed supraorbital glands that function for salt removal. A salt concentrate drains from the nares, and head shaking scatters the droplets. Moreover, populations of ducks exposed to seawater tend to have larger salt glands than their freshwater counter-parts (Cooch 1964). Individuals as well as populations respond to in-creased or decreased salinity, as shown in eiders that leave the sea to in-cubate (McArthur and Gorman 1978). Although ducks are well equipped physiologically to tolerate salt water, they seem to prefer to drink fresh water, and some well-adapted marine species such as the Falkland Kelp Sheldgoose (*Chloëphaga hybrida malvinarum*) fly considerable distances to freshwater sources (Weller 1972).

Sources of Colonizers: Migrants and Accidentals

Ornithological journals are full of records of accidentals or strays. At times it seems that more space is devoted to these than to common local birds, but these records help in the assessment of potential im-migrants to a new habitat. Some islands obviously are on "flightlines" and visitors are regular; but regardless of the remoteness of the land mass, accidentals reach it and occasionally establish a new species on an island. Some species are especially prone to dispersal and pioneering on islands; Diamond (1974) termed these "supertramps." David Lack has discussed such accidental waterfowl (1970, 1974) and land birds (1976) in relation to habitat and establishment.

The cold-temperate and subantarctic islands off the tip of South America form an interesting array of potential habitats (Fig. 1.8). Tierra del Fuego is just a few kilometers across the Magellan Strait from Patagonia, and 16 or more of the southern ducks are present there (Table 2.1). The Falkland Islands, 484 km east of the eastern tip of Patagonia and 364 km northeast of Staten Island, appear to form stepping-stones to the islands of the Scotia Arc.

Understandably, the avifauna of the Falkland Islands is South American in origin, with only one endemic species (Falkland Flightless Steamer Duck) and one unique subspecies (Falkland Kelp Sheldgoose). There are 11 regular and 4 occasional breeding anatids (Table 2.2) and at least 4 others that have been reported as accidentals (Wace 1921, Bennett 1926, Cawkell and Hamilton 1961). Although not all these records have been properly confirmed, it is clear that such accidental visits are likely. Bennett (1922) suggested that influxes were influenced by severe droughts on mainland habitats. Such responses to drought are well known in continental populations of ducks that move to suboptimal areas such as the subarctic (Hansen and McKnight 1964, Henry 1973).

TABLE 2.1

Waterfowl of Tierra del Fuego

REGULAR BREEDERS

Coscoroba (*Coscoroba coscoroba*)
Black-necked Swan (*Cygnus melanocoryphus*)
Ashy-headed Sheldgoose (*Chloëphaga poliocephala*)
Ruddy-headed Sheldgoose (*C. rubidiceps*)
Patagonian Upland Sheldgoose (*C. p. picta*)
Patagonian Kelp Sheldgoose (*C. h. hybrida*)
Magellanic Flightless Steamer Duck (*Tachyeres pteneres*)
Flying Steamer Duck (*T. patachonicus*)
Crested Duck (*Anas s. speculariodes*)
Bronze-winged Duck (*A. specularis*)
Speckled Teal (*A. f. flavirostris*)
Southern Wigeon (*A. sibilatrix*)
Brown or Yellow-billed Pintail (*A. georgica spinicauda*)
Silver Teal (*A. versicolor fretensis*)
Red Shoveler (*A. platalea*)
Torrent Duck (*Merganetta armata*)

ACCIDENTAL OR HYPOTHETICAL

White-cheeked Pintail (*A. bahamensis*)
Cinnamon Teal (*A. cyanoptera*)
Rosy-billed Pochard (*Netta peposaca*)
Peruvian Ruddy Duck (*Oxyura ferruginea*)
Argentine Ruddy Duck (*O. vittata*)

Note: Terminology after Humphrey et al. (1970) and Weller (1975a).

TABLE 2.2

Waterfowl of the Falkland Islands

REGULAR BREEDERS

Black-necked Swan (*Cygnus melanocoryphus*)
Ruddy-headed Sheldgoose (*Chloëphaga rubidiceps*)
Falkland Upland Sheldgoose (*C. picta leucoptera*)
Falkland Kelp Sheldgoose (*C. hybrida malvinarum*)
Flying Steamer Duck (*Tachyeres patachonicus*)
Falkland Flightless Steamer Duck (*T. brachypterus*)
Crested Duck (*Anas s. speculariodes*)
Southern Wigeon (*A. sibilatrix*)
Speckled Teal (*A. f. flavirostris*)
Brown or Yellow-billed Pintail (*A. georgica spinicauda*)
Silver Teal (*A. versicolor fretensis*)

OCCASIONAL BREEDERS

Coscoroba (*Coscoroba coscoroba*)
Ashy-headed Sheldgoose (*Chloëphaga poliocephala*)
Cinnamon Teal (*A. cyanoptera*)
Red Shoveler (*A. platalea*)

ACCIDENTALS

White-cheeked Pintail (*A. bahamensis*)
Rosy-billed Pochard (*Netta peposaca*)
Black-headed Duck (*Heteronetta atricapilla*)
Argentine Ruddy Duck (*Oxyura vittata*)

South Georgia, 1348 km east of the Falkland Islands, had until recently only one resident duck species, the South Georgia Pintail. The Speckled Teal has become a breeding bird at South Georgia, possibly only a few years before discovery in 1971 (Weller and Howard 1972). Single individuals of the Southern Wigeon (*Anas sibilatrix*) and the North American Blue-winged Teal were observed on South Georgia in 1972 by Andrew Clarke (pers. commun.) of the British Antarctic Survey; the latter certainly must be a long-distance record for ducks even though migrants have been taken in Argentina (Navas 1961, Storer and Gill 1961).

A duck believed to be a pintail was seen at Signy Island in the South Orkneys at lat. 60°43′ S (Fig. 1.8) (Burton 1967) as was a Southern Wigeon (Beck 1968). An emaciated Black-necked Swan (*Cygnus melanocoryphus*) was found dead near the Antarctic Peninsula, and a Brown Pintail was collected at Deception Island in the South Shetlands at lat. 62°59′ S. A most surprising record is that of the Argentine Ruddy Duck (*Oxyura vittata*) on Deception Island in the South Shetlands. This is another record thought to be drought induced (Bennett 1920). Another unidentified pintail was seen by David Parmelee on Breaker Island near Anvers Island at lat. 64°50′ S (Palmer Peninsula, Antarctica) in mid-spring 1975 (Watson 1975). Because of prevailing westerlies in this area, I think it unlikely that this bird came from the South Georgia population.

Another interesting record is of Black-necked Swans shot on Juan Fernandez Island (Lönnberg 1920). Presumably, these came from Chile, a minimal westerly movement of 650 km.

Tristan da Cunha is a very remote island in the South Atlantic (lat. 37°15′ S), of recent volcanic origin, abrupt, and with little standing water (Baker et al. 1964). It is isolated from Africa by 2800 km and from South America by 3200 km, but with prevailing westerlies its avifauna is essentially American in origin (Rand 1955). The ability of ducks to reach this isolated island is shown by sighting of "teal" in the area, but no breeding ducks have become established (Elliot 1953).

Another subantarctic island with a recorded history of waterfowl pioneering is Macquarie Island, 824 km southeast of Tasmania and 374 km southwest of the Auckland Islands (Fig. 1.10). A population of Gray Ducks has become established within the present century (Carrick 1957, Warham 1969). Gray Teal (Keith and Hines 1958) and Mallards were first seen in 1949 (Gwynn 1953), the latter obviously derived from stock introduced in New Zealand or Australia, and they are still seen occasionally (Merilees 1971).

As a series of large and remote land masses, New Zealand has essentially an island avifauna, and potential colonizers are common. Although there are only seven extant native ducks and one extinct endemic, at least seven other Australian species are accidental or casuals or have pioneered briefly and died out (Table 2.3). Hutton (1873) early

TABLE 2.3
Waterfowl of New Zealand

REGULAR BREEDERS
New Zealand Shelduck or Paradise Duck (*Tadorna variegata*)
Blue Mountain Duck (*Hymenolaimus malacorhynchos*)
Gray Teal (*Anas gibberifrons*)
Brown Teal (*A. aucklandica chlorotis*)
New Zealand Gray Duck (*A. s. superciliosa*)
New Zealand Shoveler (*A. rhynchotis variegata*)
New Zealand Scaup (*Aythya novae-seelandiae*)

SUCCESSFUL INTRODUCTIONS
Mute Swan (*Cygnus olor*)
Black Swan (*C. atratus*)
Canada Goose (*Branta canadensis*)
Mallard (*Anas platyrhynchos*)

PIONEERED NATURALLY AND DISAPPEARED
Plumed Whistling Duck (*Dendrocygna eytoni*)
Cape Barren Goose (*Cereopsis novae-hollandiae*)
Maned Goose or Australian Wood Duck (*Chenonetta jubata*)
Australian Shoveler (*A. r. rhynchotis*)
Pink-eared Duck (*Malacorhynchus membranaceus*)
Australian White-eye (*Aythya australis*)
Musk Duck (*Biziura lobata*)

EXTINCT
Auckland Merganser (*Mergus australis*)

Note: Terminology after Hutton (1871), Falla (1953), Williams (1962), Fleming (1962), Williams (1968), and Kear and Scarlett (1970).

noted the uniqueness of endemic New Zealand waterfowl and pointed out that stray Tufted Ducks reported on Pacific islands could explain how northern ducks could have become established in New Zealand, giving rise to New Zealand Scaup. The accidental occurrence of North American Blue-winged Teal in Argentina and recently in South Georgia demonstrates that such hemispheric shifts can occur, even though teal are not yet established as breeding birds.

Tropical islands also are visited regularly by northern ducks. A number of North American species regularly winter on the Hawaiian Islands: Pintails, Common Shoveler (*Anas clypeata*), American Wigeon (*A. americana*), and Lesser Scaup. Accidentals in the Hawaiian chain are numerous: Lesser Snow Goose (*A. caerulescens*), Cackling Canada Goose, Black Brant (*B. bernicla orientalis*), White-fronted Goose (*Anser albifrons*), Emperor Goose (*A. canagicus*), Red-breasted Merganser, Hooded Merganser (*Mergus cucullatus*), Bufflehead (*Bucephala albeola*), Gadwalls, Mallards, North American Green-winged Teal (*Anas crecca carolinensis*), Blue-winged Teal, Redhead, Ring-necked Duck (*A. collaris*), Canvasback (*A. valisineria*), Greater Scaup, Old Squaw (*Clangula hyemalis*), Surf Scoter (*Melanitta perspicillata*), Harlequin (*Histrionicus histrionicus*), and North American Ruddy Duck (*Oxyura j.*

jamaicensis) (Bryan 1901, Bryan and Greenway 1944, Udvardy 1961, Berger 1972). European ducks also occur: European Wigeon (*Anas penelope*), Tufted Duck, Garganey (*Anas querguedula*), European Green-winged Teal (*A. c. crecca*) (Clapp and Woodward 1968, Ely and Clapp 1973). Shovelers, northern Pintails, Gadwalls, and Mallards could come from either Asia or North America. The White-fronted Goose, taken on Midway Island at the west end of the Hawaiian chain, also could have come from either continent (Fisher 1965).

Eurasian migrants regularly reach Indian Ocean islands. European Green-winged Teal, Mallards, European Wigeons, Gadwalls, Common White-eyes, and Garganey are known from Socotra Island (Ripley and Bond 1966). Garganey and Tufted Ducks are known from the Maldive Islands (Watson et al. 1963).

With time and the inherent propensities for dispersal, potential inhabitants could arrive on any island. Why migrants would remain on remote islands is uncertain. Because few ducks cross the equator in regular latitudinal migration, navigation may not be as efficient as for some shorebirds that regularly shift from one hemisphere to the other. Johnston and McFarlane (1967) suggested that physical condition influenced whether or not Golden Plovers (*Pluvialis dominica*) left Wake Island for the migration north to breed; birds in poor condition did not migrate.

Island Size and Remoteness

With the capacity of birds to fly long distances and reach remote places, what factors influence the rate at which arrival and establishment occur? MacArthur and Wilson (1967) considered the importance of both geographic and ecological influences on avifaunas, but these and numerous subsequent authors have emphasized the larger terrestrial faunas rather than ducks or other waterbirds.

Island ("target") size may influence the chances that emigrants radiating from a given point will make a landing, but more importantly, island area influences the number of species that can exist there. In an analysis of the resident freshwater birds of four islands I have studied (Table 2.4, and Fig. 2.1), the regression between island size (area) and number of species is statistically significant at the 0.05 level ($R^2 = 0.9360$; $F = 29.27$). However, a similar analysis for all birds found on these islands is not quite significant ($R^2 = 0.8772$; $F = 14.28$) because of the different patterns found in birds of different habitats. An analysis of waterfowl by continent or zoogeographic region (Fig. 2.2) shows a significant correlation between number of breeding species and

TABLE 2.4

Differences in bird species richness on four subantarctic islands in relation to size, distance from source fauna, and habitat

Habitat	Tierra del Fuego		Falklands		Aucklands		South Georgia		Significance	
	No.	%	No.	%	No.	%	No.	%	Area	Distance
Marine	10	10	25	41	23	55	22	84	<0.05	N.S.
Freshwater	33	32	14	23	3	7	2	8	<0.05	N.S.
Terrestrial	59	58	22	36	16	38	2	8	<0.05	<0.05
Total	102		61		42		26		N.S.	N.S.
Area (km^2)	71,162		11,960		606		3756			
Distance from source (km)	5		364		456		1718			

Note: N.S. = not significant.

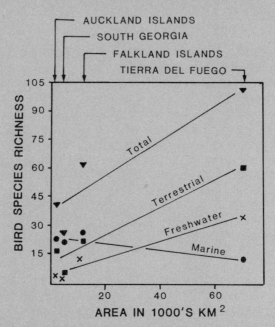

Fig. 2.1. Relationship between the area of four southern islands and number of species (species richness) breeding there according to habitats.

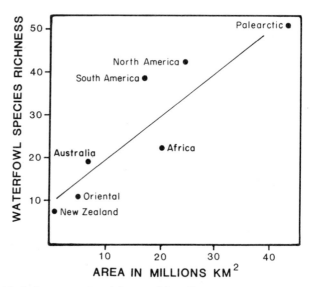

Fig. 2.2. Relationship between species richness of breeding waterfowl and continent or region size (Africa corrected for the Sahara Desert).

region size ($R^2 = 0.6622; F = 9.802; P = <0.05$). If Africa is corrected by eliminating the Sahara Desert, the correlation is still greater ($R^2 = 0.7834; F = 18.078; P = <.01$).

Although there seems to be a relationship between remoteness and reduced resident bird species (Table 2.4) or freshwater birds alone, these data are not statistically significant, since they are complicated by size and habitat preference. However, species richness of terrestrial birds alone is significantly and inversely correlated with island distance from source faunas and area ($R^2 = 0.9996; F = 1154.798; P = <0.05$) or distance alone if distance data are squared ($R^2 = 0.9996; F = 1183.298; P = <0.05$).

These data suggest that the more remote islands are more difficult for terrestrial birds to reach and adapt to, but marine or freshwater birds are less influenced by distance. Nevertheless, distance induces sedentary populations because of the difficulty of their periodic return to the mainland. Some islands such as Ireland and Britain have a sufficiently mild climate that breeding species could also overwinter, but such islands seem not to provide sufficient isolation to produce endemics. There is genetic mixing via ingress of birds that may stay and breed, and locally reared birds move short distances to larger and more diverse habitats for winter resources. However, Vancouver Island and other coastal islands of Canada and Alaska are even nearer to the continent than Ireland and England but support an endemic race of Canada Goose (*Branta canadensis fulva*). Family social structure may be a strong influence on such differentiation, as noted by Mayr (1942) in the Canada Goose.

The nearest island with an endemic anatid is Cuba, about 210 km from Yucatan and 230 km from Florida. Here the Cuban or Black-billed Whistling Duck may be ecologically isolated by habitat availability. The Falkland Islands are not much farther from South America (a minimum of 364 km), but strong, opposing, and erratic winds are common. The Auckland Islands are only 456 km south of New Zealand (373 km south of Stewart Island), but precise orientation would be required to return to the mainland; the climatic conditions of the "Roaring Forties" are so variable that an annual migration is less feasible than adjusting to the relatively moderate winter conditions on the islands. Thus islands from 200 km to 500 km from the mainland, with a sufficiently moderate climate to permit survival over the winter, seem to form potential habitats for pioneering stock and subsequent genetic isolation.

The most remote islands are perhaps Tristan da Cunha and the Hawaiian chain, which at the shortest distance would be nearly 2800 km from the nearest stock of potential migrants. Although ducks have been sighted at Tristan, little wetland habitat is present and no ducks have become established. Distance obviously has not prevented the establishment of resident populations on the Hawaiian Islands and other remote

Pacific archipelagoes. Kerguelen Island is 3800 km from Africa, but the Prince Edward and Crozet islands are about 1736 km and 2528 km from Africa respectively and may have formed stepping-stones.

Even where islands are not remote, pioneers preadapted to certain habitat conditions probably move to such areas on larger islands and become ecologically as well as geographically isolated. For example, Salvadori's Duck of New Guinea seems to be isolated in highland streams and lakes (Mayr and Rand 1937, Gyldenstolpe 1955, Hitchcock 1964, Rand and Gilliard 1967, Kear 1975), so the forest zone effectively forms an ecological barrier against movement to other islands or invading species. Numerous South American subspecies reside in the high Andes and also are isolated on "ecological islands."

Wind and Spatial Relationships

Most endemic island waterfowl occur on islands located east or south of the source area. Because of the dominance of westerly winds in the south-temperate and subantarctic regions (Fig. 2.3) either normal or violent winds may direct birds to specific islands. Westerlies are regular off the tip of South America, and eastward flights to the Falkland Islands and from there to South Georgia are logical. Tickell (1965) discussed the storm front that preceded sighting of a Common Egret (*Casmerodius albus*) on South Georgia, an event that must occur regularly with a variety of birds. Barn swallows (*Hirundo rustica*) and Chilean Swallows (*Tachycineta leucopyga*) are seen annually on the Falkland Islands but do not survive because of the high winds and lack of flying insects (Cawkell and Hamilton 1961).

Wind systems that might move ducks from Australia toward New Zealand or on to the Auckland Islands occur with sufficient regularity that dispersal would seem to be no problem. It is possible that immigrants directly from Australia could reach the Auckland and Campbell islands, since sightings of Australian birds in New Zealand often are on the southwest coast of South Island rather than North Island (see Williams 1968).

However, it is obvious that some ducks from the northern hemisphere have reached New Zealand without recorded establishment in Australia or intermediate small islands, giving rise to the New Zealand Scaup and Auckland Merganser. The Tufted Duck (Hutton 1871) and the Chinese Merganser or Common Merganser (Humphrey 1955) are the presumed ancestors of these distinctive species. Such shifting between hemispheres may have taken place during the Pleistocene, when northern breeding areas must have been well south of present locations.

Indian Ocean Pintails now isolated on islands at lat. 45° to 50° S are

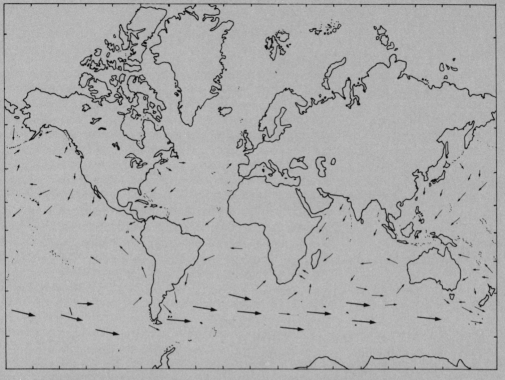

Fig. 2.3. Major wind directions in the southern hemisphere
(after Espenshade 1970).

derived from northern Pintails that nest up to lat. 82° N (Palmer 1976a).
Wind patterns from weather atlases and wind roses for the Kerguelen
Islands (Fabricius 1957) suggest that northwesterly winds occasionally
favor movement to the southeast (see Fig. 2.3). Winds from India
sometimes are suitable, but movement from South Africa seems more
likely. It is interesting that no duck populations became established
naturally on Amsterdam or St. Paul islands northeast of the Kerguelen
Islands. These apparently lie in the southeast trade winds, and such air
masses would oppose birds moving from the west. The fact that the
Kerguelen form (*A. eatoni*) has been artificially introduced on both
islands suggests that habitats were adequate to support immigrants but
that none had yet reached there.

The Galapagos Pintail obviously became established from stock that
moved westward. Because of the dominance of the northeast trade winds
it is probable that birds originated from northern South America. Northwesterly winds off the west coast of South America also are common
(Fig. 2.3). Nearctic Blue-winged Teal are occasional migrants in the
Galapagos, demonstrating that this type of movement occurs.

The tropical Pacific endemics could have been derived from Nearctic migrants from the northeast or north or from Palearctic migrants from the northwest. Present-day migrants and accidentals recorded on Hawaii and still more southerly islands suggest a Nearctic origin, and distances and wind systems also favor origin from the northwest coast of North America or the Aleutian Islands, a south or southwesterly movement of about 3800 km.

Establishment and Island Environments

The wanderings of strong flying ducks eventually should permit their arrival at any island regardless of its size or remoteness, but survival there depends on the island as a habitat. Gross climatic and geological conditions as they influence the development of wetlands and wetland biotas, morphology of rivers and seashores, characteristics of vegetation, and relative abundance of food items all play a vital role in the evolution of suitable conditions for waterfowl. Mineral composition and age of islands influence the availablility of nutrients and development of productive wetlands.

Some islands even 300 km to 500 km off shore are of continental shelf origin, while most remote ones are of volcanic origin (Fosberg 1966). Post-Pleistocene surfaces of volcanic islands such as the Galapagos (Williams 1966) are suitable for ducks mainly because of the availability of coastal lagoons, but sphagnum bog areas produced by higher moisture levels at high altitudes are also present (Colinvaux 1968). Similar bogs occur on Washington Island, once inhabited by a Gadwall, and on Hawaiian Islands such as Kauai. Sandy atolls would seem to be the least suitable for ducks, but the Laysan Teal resides on one; however, the species may have had a wider range at one time.

Temperature is a major influence on habitat quality because it affects the rate of chemical and biological processes, and such factors produce a slower rate of evolution in polar ecosystems (Dunbar 1968) and impact on the suitability of habitats for waterfowl, especially on islands. Subantarctic islands such as South Georgia were influenced by and are just emerging from extensive Pleistocene glaciation. Peat beds dated to 1843 years on Signy Island (Godman and Switsur 1966) are the best measure of conditions suitable for terrestrial or freshwater birds at this latitude. The resulting glacial tarns and coastal barrier ponds built of alluvium make suitable breeding areas for South Georgia Pintails, but species requiring larger invertebrates as food probably could not survive there (Weller 1975b).

The distribution of vegetation suitable for nesting or predator pro-

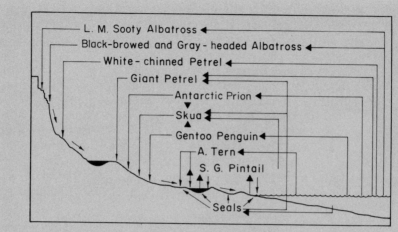

Fig. 2.4.   Hypothetical pattern of nutrient flow from the sea to the coastal area of South Georgia.

tection may not be a problem on most tropical islands, but it is a serious one in the rugged environments of subantarctic islands. Areas like South Georgia are either ice, rock, or glacial debris over nine-tenths of their surfaces, and only shorelines near the sea have extensive vegetation of tussock (*Poa flabellata*) and other grasses suitable as nest and brood cover. These shorelines may be rich only because of avian and mammalian transport of nutrients from the sea; hence, the presence of cover for ducks actually may result from the presence of breeding albatrosses or petrels and basking seals (Holdgate 1960, 1967; Weller 1975c). Duck foods in the lakes undoubtedly are also influenced by nutrient enrichment from seabirds and seals. These theoretical relationships are shown schematically in Figure 2.4.

Foods providing nutrition for body maintenance or for the special high-protein demands of laying females must either be present on the island or the pioneer must be such a generalist that it can use what is present. Lack (1970) pointed out that most island isolates are derived from dabbling ducks of the genus *Anas* that can feed on seeds, plant material, or invertebrates. This is true, but recent studies have demonstrated that these ducks need invertebrate foods for laying eggs and that most actually use them in the prelaying period (see e.g., Swanson and Nelson 1970, Krapu 1974). Moreover, most subantarctic or even cold-temperate islands have few native terrestrial plants with seeds large enough to serve as a major food resource. It is obvious that ecologically more "mature" islands with greater diversity of food resources not only can support more individuals but may have greater potential for species specializing on different foods. This concept will be related later to the evolution of species complexes on islands.

The cold-temperate and subantarctic ducks that I have collected during the austral summer have all been feeding more on animal material than on plant material. Fresh water is the initial preference of most species, but Flightless Teal feed at the seashores on Mollusca, Isopoda, and Amphipoda (Weller 1975d). South Georgia Pintails shift from fresh water to salt water freely (Weller 1975c). The description of foods taken by Kerguelen Pintails (Paulian 1953) suggests similar behavior. Few data are available on marine feeding by tropical species, but Hawaiian Ducks do use estuaries and even "salt ponds" and Laysan Teal feed in a hypersaline lagoon.

Initial success on islands with limited fresh water often may stem from preadaptation of ducks to tolerate saline conditions such as they find in estuaries or protected seashores. However, reproductive success ultimately will depend on production and survival of the ducklings. Few species of island ducks actually rear their young in salt water on marine foods; but salinity alone may not be the major factor, since alkaline ponds in desert areas often are favored rearing ponds. However, the presence of fresh water of some type is essential to most ducks in their initial colonization, and most still use it. South Georgia Pintails, for example, seem to rear their young only on freshwater ponds, although adults and mature ducklings feed on the shores of fjords or the sea.

In the subantarctic climate, the availability of warm and protected waters in summer with a suitable diversity of invertebrates essential to growth may be the most important influence on survival. In an area of milder climate Auckland Flightless Teal seem to be entirely seashore birds during the breeding and postbreeding season, but they do use fresh water for drinking as do even the most marine of all anatids, the Steamer Ducks and Kelp Sheldgeese of the Magellanic region. If Auckland Flightless Teal indeed, evolved from isolated Brown Teal or their common ancestors, the presence of estuary-dwelling populations on outlying islands of New Zealand may have been the source of the immigrants; this preadaptation may have been significant in their successful colonization of the Auckland Islands.

Most endemic island waterfowl are found on tropical or southern oceanic cold-temperate islands, but a few subspecies occur in northern latitudes. Monthly means of air temperature of several subantarctic islands (Fig. 2.5) show relative temperature stability. This feature is expected in the tropics but also occurs in the cold-temperate region because of the oceanic influence on relatively small land masses. The mean temperature is merely lower, but all cold-temperate to subantarctic areas

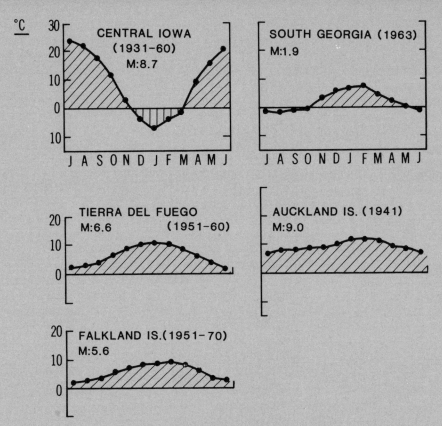

Fig. 2.5. Seasonal variation in temperature on several major subantarctic islands compared to that of central Iowa.

with resident ducks have temperature regimes that permit freshwater feeding for at least five or six months and the use of open seashores the remainder of the year.

Air temperature is also a factor needing much study in relation to bioenergetics of birds. However, on the basis of breeding areas of ducks in Arctic areas in summer and the northern limits of their wintering areas in the northern hemisphere, the temperature regimes of subantarctic islands would not overly tax ducks if a suitable food supply were present. Ducks often winter in places where air temperature is constantly below freezing but the water is kept ice-free by thermal pollution or natural warm springs. But in addition to body maintenance females must metabolize sufficient reserves for egg development, which may be difficult with severely cold air temperatures. Establishing this energy balance may be impossible in some areas that have wetland habitats but a colder winter climate than South Georgia such as, for example, Signy Island (Heywood 1967).

Temperatures of the midcontinental United States (see Iowa example in Fig. 2.5) demonstrate the difficulty of survival of aquatic birds in midwinter under still more severe conditions. Temperature clearly is a meaningful factor in determining what areas can support sedentary populations through the winter.

The physical and biological limits of adaptation by ducks to the subantarctic are shown by pintails. Indian Ocean Pintails apparently are strong fliers and are doing well on Kerguelen Island, less than 600 km from Heard Island. Whereas Kerguelen Island has areas that are moist, well watered, and of diverse altitudes and habitats, Heard Island is a much-glaciated volcanic cone with abrupt cliffs and reduced wetlands. Like South Georgia, Heard Island is nine-tenths ice and snow covered. It also has a more severe climate than Kerguelen, being well within the Antarctic Convergence. Ealey (1954) suggested that all life had been eliminated on Heard in the Pleistocene, but the island has been repopulated during the past 15,000 years. Presumably the Kerguelen Pintail could (and perhaps has) reached Heard Island, but it has not become established there. If straying Kerguelen Pintails reach Heard Island, will the factor limiting establishment be a shortage of suitable fresh water for rearing of ducklings or will it be a shortage of marine food resources suitable to hold birds through winter conditions that average 3°C colder than Kerguelen (climatic data from Fabricius 1957)?

The most extreme conditions of a duck-inhabited island are those of South Georgia, where warm freshwater ponds are available in summer but freezing temperatures force birds to feed on seashores all winter and occasionally at any time of year (Matthews 1951, Weller 1975c). Both pond and seashore conditions may limit food resources on Heard Island. Wetlands are scarce, so any sizable population would be forced to use the seashore even for rearing young. However, based on the work of Koskimies and Lahti (1964), it may be impossible for newly hatched ducklings to survive in ocean waters within the Antarctic Convergence. These authors found that survival of ducklings is inhibited by cold and that in northern Europe latitudinal ranges of breeding ducks correlate with the tolerance of ducklings to cold.

Even if warmer, freshwater ponds are present, waterfowl seem restricted in their polar distribution by the availability of ice-free conditions in winter. Where temperatures are sufficiently severe that ponds freeze, ducks must move to estuaries and seashores. Thus while Pintails can survive on Kerguelen Island or South Georgia, it is unlikely that they can overwinter on Heard Island, Signy Island, or the Argentine islands of the Antarctic Peninsula with the ice pack along the shores during winter. Because wind conditions reduce the feasibility of annual migrations, the establishment of breeding ducks on such isolated and severe habitats is unlikely.

CHAPTER 3

Responses to Island Living

Flightlessness

NOMADIC or migratory movements of ducks and other birds are a product of necessity, accident, or advantage made possible by strong powers of flight. Flight may be a disadvantage on islands. Although most species of island ducks can still fly, some rarely do so. Moreover, biochemical evidence exists that flight capabilities are reduced via physiological modifications. Laysan Teal, for example, have muscle-enzyme systems more comparable to nonflying domestic Mallards than wild ones (Kaplan 1964). There is no good evidence that any island endemic makes regular migrations to nearby continents. Olrog (1948) suggested that the Falkland Kelp Sheldgoose winters along the coast of Tierra del Fuego, but this has not been adequately documented. There are certainly seasonal population shifts of Kelp Sheldgeese in the Magellanic region, but whether this involves Falkland birds needs to be proven. Unlike continental races of ducks commonly reported as accidentals on islands, the reverse situation is rarely recorded. A Hawaiian Duck has been recorded as being taken in Mexico (Leopold 1972), but a strong likelihood of a labeling error exists.

Reduced mobility in island birds obviously conserves individuals of the island population, since undue losses would be experienced by migratory or nomadic behavior (Miller 1966, MacArthur and Wilson 1967). Many island species still capable of flight show reduced flight tendencies and, eventually, inability to fly. Reduced numbers of flight feathers already occur in Laysan Teal, and reduced wing size (and number of flight feathers) is the next step, as in the Auckland Flightless Teal (Gadow 1902) and flightless steamer ducks (Fig. 3.1). Such reduced wings are, however, highly efficient for flapping escape in these birds. Moreover, there are other advantages to reduced wing size. Olson (1973), speaking of island rails, suggested that the maintenance of large flight

55

Fig. 3.1. Auckland Flightless Teal, showing poorly developed wings and eye-ring.

muscles is inefficient use of energy and is selected against when flight offers few other advantages. It has been suggested that reduced wings may improve body contour and diving efficiency in steamer ducks or may provide a smoother outline for birds like Flightless Teal that walk through dense vegetation and move in and out of burrows made by petrels or rabbits (Weller 1975d).

Terrestrial behavior is a striking feature of many endemic ducks on small islands, and information on others may not have been recorded because this behavior is difficult to quantify and separate from tameness and curiosity. Most workers have been impressed by the hesitancy of island ducks to take flight even when pressed. Reischek (1889) noted that pursued Auckland Mergansers sought refuge by hiding among rocks rather than diving as northern mergansers do. Fisher (1903) noted that Laysan Teal walked in preference to flying. Kidder (1875) observed that Kerguelen Pintails "walked along the ground like quails with little of the waddle of ducks." Sclater and Salvin (1878) reported Kerguelen Pintails running or walking in rows to inspect their collector Moseley, and Murphy (1916) and I have had similar experiences with South Georgia Pintails. As implied above, the terrestrial behavior of Flightless Teal is greatly developed. Additional terrestrial behavior related to feeding will be considered elsewhere.

That terrestrial behavior has reduced the efficiency of some ducks as well-adapted waterbirds has been implied by some observations. Laysan Teal apparently become drenched in tropical rains (Warner 1963). Although marine-dwelling Auckland Flightless Teal do swim and even dive a great deal, they do so only for short periods, during which time their plumage becomes very soggy. They spend much of their time in preening. Both species bathe in salt water.

Marine Adaptations

Behavioral adaptations to the sea are common, especially when marine foods are a regular part of the diet. Wave avoidance is common among South Georgia Pintails and Auckland Flightless Teal. South Georgia Pintails tend to feed at sea in quiet areas, never under stormy conditions. When they feed in the shallows where surf pounding could be a problem, they turn into each incoming wave to avoid being overwashed. Auckland Flightless Teal are still better adapted to the sea but are always cautious with heavy surf. They also feed mostly in sheltered areas; but when driven to swim along the coast, they rush through the surf zone to waters quieted by floating marine algae and then swim parallel to the shore. At the point where they wish to land, they charge forward with the waves, occasionally being tossed ashore by the force of an incoming breaker and respond to the ordeal with a rapid rearrangement of feathers. Falkland Flightless Steamer Ducks are adapted to the sea by means of morphology as well as behavior. Their large size, massive structure, and diving efficiency permit use of deeper water zones where turbulence is less than that occurring along the coast. Even their ducklings can survive stormy turbulence that would deter or even damage adults of other smaller species.

Tidal rhythms are another marine feature to which freshwater birds must adapt. In the northern hemisphere, several continental species of waterfowl have evolved in association with the coastlines and estuaries. Brant feed during low tides (Einarsen 1965), and Common Shelducks (*Tadorna tadorna*) change their time and manner of feeding according to the tide, since it influences the availability of their foods in estuaries (Bryant and Leng 1975). Numerous other ducks that use estuaries must be equally flexible. Among waterfowl, Falkland Kelp Sheldgeese are one of the best adapted to the seashore and feed on algae at low tide. Normally, they walk on exposed outcrops, but on several occasions I have seen birds at the time of the falling tide swim to still-submerged feeding sites and with head and neck under water seek the algae. Numerous Brown Teal on Great Barrier Island of New Zealand feed mainly by dabbling in shallow edges at low tide and move to and from these feeding areas punctually (Weller 1974). Flightless Teal also feed by dabbling at low tide, but at other times of day they dive or feed by other methods. Obviously, if major foods are derived from the sea, digestive rhythms must either adapt to this forced feeding pattern, or physiological drives may induce terrestrial feeding, as is common in both Brown Teal and Auckland Flightless Teal.

Predators

Because of the usual absence of mammalian predators on remote islands, ducks moving from a continent to an island decrease the types of predators to which they are exposed. However, avian predators on islands may be more adaptable in diet in an area of reduced prey diversity.

Although flightlessness seems to evolve mainly in the absence of ground predators, the Auckland Flightless Teal apparently does face a unique ground predator. Mammalian predators are lacking, but Brown Skuas (*Catharacta lonnbergi*) do much of their hunting from the ground at dusk (and possibly at night, because they kill several species of petrels that are night fliers). The precise method of hunting is not known, but I have commonly encountered skuas at dusk standing under a tree canopy in areas where teal and petrels walk at night. Although teal show constant fear of skuas and move to open water or burrows or crevices when they are overhead, I have never seen any more than a threat by a skua. Nevertheless, remains of adult teal appear at skua nest sites with sufficient regularity that teal obviously make up a significant portion of food for young skuas. Robertson (1976) reported remains of Campbell Flightless Teal in skua "middens."

The South Georgia Pintail and Indian Ocean Pintail also may be influenced by skua predation, and southern Black-backed Gulls (*Larus dominicus*) may be important predators also. Murphy (1916) logically assumed that skuas were the major predator on eggs and young of South Georgia Pintails, and Sclater and Salvin (1878) and Hall (1900) regarded them as the major predator of Kerguelen Pintails. I have seen skuas dive on adult South Georgia Pintails but have never seen a kill or even a strike. South Georgia Pintails also are alert to skuas overhead, but they do not show the fear that is obvious in Auckland Flightless Teal.

The young of both South Georgia Pintails and Auckland Flightless Teal are very wary. They are well camouflaged by having their ancestral yellow and black modified to dull yellow or buff and auburn-tipped sepia, similar in color to the peat soils and shaded waters. Kerguelen Pintail and Auckland Merganser young are similarly colored. Their vocalizations are soft even when they are lost from the parents, and they lack the tameness of adults.

Even adult Auckland Flightless Teal have very soft vocalizations effective for only short distances, and they lack the complex calls characteristic of displays of pintails that still fly easily. Perkins (1903) commented on the soft quality of the Hawaiian Duck's vocalization as well, but I know of no quantitative data to document these suggestions.

The vulnerability of island birds to predators is well known, and several duck species appear to be absent on islands where predators have been introduced intentionally or accidentally. The Lesser Wandering Whistling Duck seems to have been extirpated from Fiji by the introduction of the mongoose (Delacour 1954), and the Hawaiian Koloa occurs only on the mongoose-free island of Kauai. The Auckland and Campbell flightless teal occur only on islands lacking introduced cats and pigs.

Resource Use

A major reason for examining habitat use and foods of an island with a single anatid was to discover adaptations to available resources where no anatid competition existed. However, on some of these islands typical foods might be limited. The expansion of resource use to include a greater variety of foods in a broader niche ("ecological release") is characteristic of the first colonizers of any avian group (MacArthur and Wilson 1967). Unfortunately, very little work has been done on niche segregation in continental waterfowl faunas, but the work of Olney (1963; modified in Lack 1971), Szijj (1965), Dobrowolski (1969), and White and James (1978) are diverse approaches to the problem.

Lack (1970, 1974) concluded that because of the propensity toward pioneering, solitary island endemics must be filling the only available niche, or foods were scarce and the solitary resident had to use all available resources; thus only one species of duck could exist on the island. The many influences on island colonization make such situations difficult to assess. Examination of food and habitat utilization of the South Georgia Pintail is the closest personal experience I have had with a single-species island. Because the Speckled Teal has arrived only recently on the island, it is unlikely that the niche breadth of the pintail has yet changed significantly. The Indian Ocean Pintail still is a solitary species and seems to be similar in niche breadth and feeding behavior to the South Georgia Pintail (Kidder 1875, Prevost and Mougin 1970).

Foods of other solitary species have not been studied in detail, but careful observations and notes on collected birds demonstrate a major shift from solely freshwater invertebrates to both freshwater and seashore organisms and reveal extensive utilization of terrestrial foods through adaptation. Laysan Teal are among the most terrestrial of the island ducks, and at some times of the year at least, they take an estimated 95 percent of their foods on land at night (Fisher 1903, Warner 1963). Hawaiian Ducks are known to feed on earthworms (Munro 1944). New Zealand Brown Teal feed on moth larvae and perhaps beetle larvae day or night (Weller 1974). Although not solitary, Auckland Flightless Teal feed in terrestrial situations regularly, presumably on earthworms and other invertebrates (Weller 1975d). Charles Fleming (pers. commun.) saw them feeding on sheep carcasses and suspected consumption of fly larvae. However, they rarely use streams, a habitat presumably dominated by Auckland Mergansers prior to their extinction. Both South Georgia Pintails (Weller 1975c) and Kerguelen Pintails (Kidder 1875) feed on earthworms, nematodes, and other moist-soil invertebrates with a regularity far exceeding that of continental dabbling ducks (Krapu 1974). D. Parmelee (pers. commun.) observed South Georgia Pintails feeding on seal carcasses at Bird Island.

Diving for food is not rare in continental dabbling ducks and is a regular feeding method in some, but it seems to be more regular in island species. Adult South Georgia Pintails dive regularly for fairy shrimp (*Brachinecta gaini*) in ponds too deep for dabble feeding. Auckland Flightless Teal dive effectively for invertebrates and sea lettuce in shallow, protected coastal waters. Whether they dive in fresh water is unknown.

One of the unique types of feeding by South Georgia Pintails is the seeking of short, filamentous algae that adhere tightly to submerged boulders. At low tides, pintails clamber about on the slick surfaces and scrape off the algae by use of the nail at the tip of the bill. Other food-getting behavior of South Georgia Pintails is more routine, but they feed with head and neck under water in freshwater ponds and at sea, they surface nibble in water too shallow for swimming, and they root in muddy turf and feed also at the shore of the sea or a fjord by similar methods. No food resource seems to have been neglected.

These observations suggest that most solitary ducks probably include a variety of aquatic and terrestrial habitats, effectively utilizing niches normally filled by ground-dwelling birds and other ducks and even grazing on marine plants. Without question, the ducks involved have highly adaptable ancestors from unstable habitats. The "preadaptation," as Lack (1970) calls it, allows for still more rapid expansion of niche breadth and ensures survival of pioneers.

Competitors for resources such as food may be either anatid or nonanatid; other ducks would be a most significant influence because few birds have a bill so specialized for straining invertebrates and seeds from fresh water. Because of this specialization, one assumes that ducks can compete more strongly than other birds for use of the same foods in this habitat. Dependent on the geographic area, cormorants, grebes, gulls, terns, rails, shorebirds, and herons may use the same habitats as ducks. Each has its anatomical and behavioral specialization for feeding, which implies relatively little overlap in food use between families or even orders.

Overlap in feeding and possible competition may occur when a new species arriving on an island expands its habitat use to take advantage of all resources, especially when food is relatively scarce. Thus use of terrestrial foods by ducks may place them in competition with birds of other orders. Auckland Flightless Teal and Subantarctic Snipe (*Coenocorypha aucklandica*) probably both use earthworms. Native Pipits (*Anthus novae-seelandiae*) seem to take similar crustaceans and dipteran larvae from wind-rowed kelp as do Auckland Flightless Teal, and the introduced Blackbird (*Turdus merula*) and Starling (*Sturnus vulgaris*) offer new competition to both native species. I suspect that American Flamingos and Galapagos Pintails feed on similar food items in saline pools.

Chronology of Nesting

Chronology of nesting is strongly influenced by the climatic regime and is especially noticeable in seasonal-pulse areas of northern North America (Hochbaum 1944, Sowls 1955, Delacour 1964). In areas like Australia (Frith 1967) and Argentina (Weller 1968a), where climatic fluctuation is less severe, breeding may occur over a longer span and be influenced by rainfall or water levels—presumably as they relate to available food. Bimodal peaks of breeding are not uncommon in such areas.

Patterns of waterfowl on islands show less restricted breeding periods presumably because of the more stable climatic regime. Nests or broods of tropical species like the Galapagos Pintail have been recorded in every month except December by Gifford (1913), Beebe (1924), Lack (1950), Eibl-Eibesfeldt (1959), Bowman (1960), and Leveque (1964). The climate is moderated by the Humboldt current, and there is no good indication of when the most nesting occurs or whether it also is influenced by rainfall.

The Hawaiian Duck breeds year-round in the relatively stable climate of Kauai, although most seem to breed in December through May. The same species in captivity at 1950 m altitude on the island of Hawaii breeds mainly in April through June (Swedberg 1967). Nesting or brood records from Laysan Island are too few to be meaningful, but

June and July are quoted as the breeding season by most authors (Bailey 1956, Warner 1963).

South Georgia represents a cold but stable climate where breeding still seems to occur over a longer period (almost five months) than might be expected for its latitude (Weller 1975c). It is probable that this reflects the time span when fresh water may be sufficiently open for ducklings to feed and drink, and it is also the period of longer day length and higher productivity.

Published records of the breeding season in Auckland Flightless Teal are scarce, but most records are from the austral summer. The climate of the Auckland Islands is quite mild by comparison with South Georgia, and it would seem that nesting could occur nearly all year. There is evidence by Falla and Stead (1938) that males are in dull eclipse plumage in March, suggesting a postbreeding molt.

On the Falkland Islands a few species have been recorded as nesting in all months of the year (the Speckled Teal, Crested Duck [*Anas s. speculariodes*] and Falkland Flightless Steamer Duck), but there is clearly a peak of nesting in spring and early summer. Other species such as the Falkland Kelp Sheldgoose have a rather limited nesting period in mid-November that possibly is influenced by light cycles as related to algae production in tidal areas (Weller 1972).

Territoriality

The evolution of territoriality in birds seems to be most prevalent among those with dependable food resources (Horn 1968). The ultimate degree of defense and the size of the area seem related to the supply of food for rearing the young (Lack 1954). But territoriality in ducks is extremely complex, and the relative importance of male-female relationships as opposed to area or food supply is difficult to assess (McKinney 1965). During breeding, most northern hemisphere waterfowl seek isolation, but even then feeding areas may be shared (Hochbaum 1944). Loafing areas are important territorial sites, but they too may be used by several individuals during the same season (Sowls 1955). Females of most species strongly defend their own nests, however.

Because of this social structure in dabbling ducks, feeding areas are utilized by numerous individuals of a species as well as a variety of species. Nesting areas typically are more numerous, and females from a large area still can feed in the same wetland. Moreover, because of the instability of many wetlands in prime waterfowl habitats, individuals can shift feeding areas without the difficulties of reestablishing territorial boundaries each time. Even diving ducks sometimes behave in this manner, although they occur in deeper and more stable wetlands. However, river ducks like the South African Black Duck (*Anas sparsa*), which use stable stream systems (Ball et al. 1978), and geese, which utilize terrestrial systems, strongly defend a territory that includes sites for most reproductive functions. Stability of habitat, and hence food resources, clearly is important for waterfowl as for other birds.

It seems that both types of territorial behavior occur in island waterfowl. The South Georgia Pintail is similar to northern Pintails in having social display and common feeding areas. Whether or not their pair bonds are long lasting is uncertain, but they seem to flock more in winter than summer. They engage in intense courtship on water and three-bird chases and rape flights resemble those of northern Pintails (Smith 1968). The social use of feeding areas permits South Georgia Pintails to shift from fresh water to the shoreline of fjords or the coast and to make maximal use of food resources with a minimal amount of energy directed to aggression. Nesting females often avoid social gatherings in the better feeding areas, possibly resulting in dispersal of nest sites.

The system in the Auckland Flightless Teal is quite different. Only a few areas seem to be social feeding grounds in the population that lives by the sea, and these probably are suboptimal areas used by nonbreeders. Breeding pairs are highly territorial and seem to defend a linear coastal territory where they do most of their feeding. They also defend associated uplands and in this way ensure the nest site and protective cover as well as food. Battles occur along the edges of the territories and involve flapping, skittering chases, dives, and chest-to-chest fighting. Whether the defense of a linear coastal territory of 15 m to 24 m provides all the feeding terrain necessary for broods is unknown, but certainly paired males or pairs do most if not all of their feeding in these areas. How upland populations defend territories is uncertain, but they respond aggressively to recorded calls by charging through the vegetation toward the source, suggesting that they do defend terrestrial territories.

Laysan Teal also have territories, as indicated by observations of banded birds (Warner 1963). Because much of their feeding is terrestrial, it would be interesting to know their behavior at the limited freshwater areas.

Three species residing in the Falkland Islands demonstrate the linear territories of birds that feed along seashores. Crested Ducks feed on invertebrates of gravel and silt estuaries and coves (Weller 1972). The Falkland Flightless Steamer Duck defends a long shoreline that includes a gravel area where their young feed and a slope providing access to upland nesting areas for nesting females. There seems to be little territory overlap and interspecific aggression between these two species, however, perhaps because Falkland Flightless Steamer Ducks tend to use unprotected shorelines and food resources of open water. The Falkland

Kelp Sheldgoose feeds exclusively on marine algae growing on rock shelves exposed at low tide. Males are extremely aggressive in all three species. They guard the territory constantly against intraspecific intruders, while the female incubates and protects the brood after hatching.

Broods and Brood Care

My experience of trying to observe feeding behavior of ducklings of South Georgia Pintails and Auckland Flightless Teal has convinced me that selective predation pressure by skuas and perhaps Black-backed Gulls has been sufficiently severe that ducklings rarely show themselves. Ducklings are wary and secretive and feed along the edges of ponds under overhanging tussock and in tiny puddles and channels where they are not visible from above by aerial predators.

The brood behavior of tropical island ducks does not seem to have been recorded, although several broods of Galapagos Pintails have been observed. Potential predators there include the Galapagos Hawk (*Buteo galapagensis*) (probably too slow to be a serious predator), numerous gulls, and seabirds. Nothing seems to be known of brood behavior of either Laysan Teal or Hawaiian Ducks.

Although pairs often accompany broods of southern hemisphere dabbling ducks (Weller 1968a, 1975a; Siegfried 1974), this is more common in highly territorial species with long pair bonds such as Crested Ducks, Falkland Flightless Steamer Ducks, and Falkland Kelp Sheldgeese. The relationship of males to broods in island ducks has not been well recorded. Only once did I see a male with a South Georgia Pintail brood, but other workers have observed this relationship also. Males were seen near two of four Flightless Teal broods observed in the dense tussock, but no parental behavior was noted (Weller 1975d). Brock (1951) saw only females with two broods of Laysan Teal. A male was seen with the single Andaman Teal brood reported (Baker 1899).

Reproductive Rate

One of the conspicuous features of endemic island ducks is their reduced clutch size and relatively large egg size. Murphy (1916) first noted the reduced clutch of South Georgia Pintails and other island birds. Lack (1970) summarized data on a variety of duck species demonstrating a trend for island ducks to lay 2 to 8 eggs, whereas related

Clutch and brood size of some endemic island ducks compared to continental
forms

Form	Clutch			Broods		
	No.	Mean	Range	No.	Mean	Range
Northern Pintail						
Palmer 1976a	41	9.2	?	63	6.6	3–12
	196	7.9	?	38	5.2	?
	40	9.0	8–10	55,763	6.0	?
Bellrose 1976	1276	7.76	3–14	4,253	5.6	?
Indian Ocean Pintail						
Hall 1900	1	2	...	...	...	...
Prevost and Mougin 1970	?	5	3–6	...	...	...
Falla 1937	1	5	...	...	...	...
Verrill 1895	1	4	...	...	...	...
Sclater and Salvin 1878	1	5	...	...	...	...
Loranchet 1915–16	?	6	...	...	...	...
Kidder 1875	?	4–5	...	...	...	...
South Georgia Pintail						
Weller 1975c	...	...	...	5	2.2	1–4
Lönnberg 1906	?	5	...	?	5	?
Murphy 1916	1	5	...	?	5	?
Spencely 1958	2	3.5	2–5	...	...	...
Pagenstecher 1885	1	4	...	...	...	...
Rankin 1951	...	...	...	1	2	...
Von der Steinen 1890	...	...	...	1	3	...
Bahama Pintail						
Biaggi 1970	?	?	5–12	...	...	...
Palmer 1976a	2	11	...	...	...	...
Delacour 1956	...	...	6–10	...	...	...
Galapagos Pintail						
Gifford 1913	...	...	...	1	3 or 4	...
Leveque 1964	...	...	...	...	3.3	1–5
Brown Teal						
Buller 1873	?	...	5–8	...	...	...
Oliver 1955	...	...	3–4	...	...	...
Potts 1870	?	8	...	...	...	...
Edwards 1955	...	...	...	1	4	...
Kear (pers. commun.)	2	4.5	3–6	...	...	...
Flightless Teal						
Oliver 1955	...	...	3–4	...	...	...
Weller 1975d	1	4	...	6	1.3	1–2
Mallard						
Palmer 1976a	1961	8.0	?	...	...	...
Bellrose 1976	5170	9.0	1–18	2103	6.6	?
Hawaiian Duck						
Munro 1944	5	8 +	8–10	3	7	...
Richardson and Bowles 1964	3	6.7	6–8	...	...	...
Swedberg 1967	?	8.3	3–10	50	3.1	1–7
Laysan Teal						
Ripley 1960	1	5	...	...	...	...
Warner 1963	1	4	...	...	...	...
Fisher 1903	1	6	...	...	...	...
Brock 1951	...	...	...	2	3.5	3–4
Ely and Clapp 1973	2	5	4–5	15	2.7	1–6

continental forms in both hemispheres lay 8 to 11 eggs. Unfortunately, this suggestion is based on rather scanty data for southern continents, but the pattern on islands certainly is one of small clutch size (Table 3.1).

Murphy (1916) pointed out that reduced clutch size in South Georgia Pintails might be related to the severe conditions of the subantarctic. He suggested that incubation efficiency of a small clutch would be greater under rigorous conditions. A related idea may be that essential food reserves may limit the ability of the female to maintain her body condition and the increased intake essential for greater egg production as noted in northern Pintails by Krapu (1974). Neither of these ideas explains the apparent decrease of clutch size on tropical islands, unless foods are less abundant than usually assumed. However, the decrease does not seem to be as great as in the subantarctic.

A concomitant change has been a proportionate increase in egg size to body size of island forms (Lack 1968, Kear 1973). Ripley (1960) noted that although Laysan Teal have small clutches, they lay huge eggs (Table 3.2). Lack (1970) commented that larger eggs may have been favored in evolution as opposed to a large clutch size because large eggs provide greater food reserves for ducklings in a severe environment. However, there is no evidence that island ducks have proportionately greater yolk stores than continental forms.

Murphy (1916) also suggested that clutch size might be related to population losses, an idea worthy of consideration in light of present

TABLE 3.2

Egg size of some island ducks compared with continental forms

Form	No.	Width (mm)	Length (mm)
Indian Ocean Pintail			
Prevost and Mougin 1970	?	37.5 (36–39.0)	53.8 (52.0–56.0)
Falla 1937	5	37.8 (36–39)	53.6 (52–56)
Verrill 1895	4	36.5 (35.1–37.8)	51.6 (49.8–53.6)
Loranchet 1915–16	6	36	51
Cabanis and Reichenow 1876	?	34.5–37.6	49.8–53.4
Estimated Median		36.7	52.20
Northern Pintail			
Palmer 1976a	20	37.88 ± 1.17	53.74 ± 1.23
Laysan Teal			
Fisher 1903	?	38	55
Hawaiian Duck (Koloa)			
Munro 1944	?	32.8	53.8
Weller unpubl.	2	36.4–38.6	47.5–48.2
Mallard			
Palmer 1976a	20	41.69 ± 1.03	58.12 ± 1.92
Flightless Teal			
Oliver 1955	?	44.5 (43.0–46.0)	63.0 (61.0–65.0)
Weller 1975d	4	44.2 (43.5–44.6)	65.0 (63.9–65.7)
Brown Teal			
Oliver 1955	?	42.5 (42–43)	61.5 (61–62)

concepts of population ecology. Theoretically, reproductive rate should increase in pioneering populations ("r" selection) and decline after the population fills the available habitat ("K" selection) (MacArthur and Wilson 1967). Cody (1966) attributes reduced clutch size to stable environmental conditions, as found either in the tropics or on islands. Presumably, few opportunities exist to study clutch size of species that have recently arrived; hence, Speckled Teal on South Georgia and Gray Ducks or Gray Teal on Macquarie Island are worthy of continuous observation. Unfortunately, we really do not have a good assessment of the population structure, production, and dynamics of any island duck. A five-year banding and color-marking study would yield great benefits in demonstrating longevity, movements, percent of the population breeding, number of broods per year, and age-related productivity. Until this is done, no meaningful comparison of island and continental species can be made.

Another weakness is that no data are available on reproductive rates of tropical ducks, but it appears that areas of high waterfowl species richness and numbers are unstable temperate steppes (Weller 1975e). Tropical areas may have lower population density but greater population stability. If this is true, the stability of island climate and sedentary populations may be factors in the apparent low reproductive rates.

A possible example of artificially induced competition between species with different reproductive rates stabilized by long periods of evolution in different habitats is found in the introduction of Mallards into New Zealand. Mallards apparently outcompete the native Gray Ducks by virtue of larger clutches, more successful rearing of large broods, and possibly a higher rate of breeding effort by all age groups (Williams and Roderick 1973). As a result some biologists are concerned over potential loss of the Gray Duck due to productivity of the Mallard and hybridization. This may ultimately prove a most valuable but unfortunate experiment.

Plumage Changes

One of my interests in island ducks was to gain insight into the basic differences in plumage patterns that are characteristic of northern hemisphere versus southern hemisphere ducks. I have attempted to summarize and classify some of these patterns elsewhere (Weller 1968a). Lack (1970) has summarized some key references relating to the speculations concerning the importance of sexual dichromatism in northern hemisphere anatids compared to island forms. Most workers suggest that monochromatism (Fig. 3.2) is a primitive character in ducks comparable

Fig. 3.2. Two male South Georgia Pintails and a female, showing general monochromatism of plumage but larger body size and head shape of the male.

to that in geese (Kear 1970). Others have suggested that the brilliant plumages of northern male anatids are related more to interspecific reproductive isolation than to sex recognition.

Isolated island forms lacking species interactions presumably lose the bright plumage because of the selective disadvantage in predation (Sibley 1957, Lack 1970). Classical examples would be the dulled (eclipselike) breeding plumages of the males of the Pacific island Mallard, Washington Gadwall, and Indian Ocean Pintail (Sibley 1957). But this does not explain the absence of sexual dichromatism in many species on southern continents. These could be ancient forms that, like geese, have never evolved the secondary bright plumages, or could be forms that were derived from northern ancestors that have lost their plumage dimorphism as endemic island waterfowl have.

The nature of the pair bonds is an important aspect of plumage dimorphism, for it is generally the species with long pair bonds that lack dichromatism. But other factors such as the chronology of breeding also are involved. In the northern hemisphere, seasonality is so pronounced and so regular that long-distance migration is common, postmolting dispersal is regular, and long pair bonds offer fewer benefits than disadvantages. New mates are sought annually. The social and competitive interactions of males may relate to this competition for females in populations where female mortality normally exceeds that of males (Sibley 1957). Sex ratios of island ducks are unknown, but reduced terrestrial nest predators may cause less pressure on females.

On islands and in warmer or stabler climates, less mobility occurs, pair bonds are long, and brood care by males is more common. Brilliant plumage presumably makes birds more vulnerable to predators and provides less advantage than disadvantage.

Still another influence may be variability in the breeding season. It has been suggested elsewhere that breeding seasons in South America are variable and it would be disadvantageous if plumage cycles and nesting opportunities did not coincide in sexually and seasonally dichromatic species (Weller 1968a). However, Siegfried (1974) was unable to gather support data from African anatids for this theory.

Although some southern hemisphere ducks are sexually dichromatic, most are of the permanently rather than seasonally dichromatic type (i.e., there is no seasonal change) (Fig. 3.3). Exceptions occur in the stifftails throughout the world and in New Zealand Shovelers (*Anas rhynchotis variegata*). In either dichromatic or brightly colored monomorphic forms, however, there is a tendency for southern anatids to have plain-colored feathers rather than the vermiculated, barred, or spotted feathers common to northern male dabbling ducks. There are exceptions, and these tend to be in Australia and New Zealand where seasonality is somewhat increased by virtue of latitude.

All northern ducks appear to have two molts per year—a complete molt following breeding that involves body, wings, and tail and a partial molt involving only the body (occasionally body and tail). The double body molt is found even in monomorphic forms in the southern hemisphere as demonstrated by Falla and Stead (1938) for New Zealand, Frith (1967) for Australia, and Weller (1968a) for Argentina. Only a few cases of double wing molt have been recorded in the stifftails (Humphrey and Clark 1964, Siegfried 1970, Johnsgard 1975, Palmer 1976b).

Among island ducks, Auckland Flightless Teal have a clear-cut double molt with a dull plumage in males during nonbreeding periods (Falla and Stead 1938). South Georgia Pintails have two plumages, but the lack of sexual and seasonal dichromatism except in the specula makes this change conspicuous more by the molting than by plumage color (Weller 1975d). Kerguelen and Crozet pintails also have duller nonbreeding plumages, essentially lacking vermiculation in males.

All males of island ducks originating from northern anatids

Fig. 3.3. Pair of Kelp Sheldgeese showing dramatic permanent (i.e., year-round) sexual dichromatism. The white male is conspicuous anyplace in its territory; the female is well camouflaged when feeding or on the nest.

(Mallards, Pintails, Gadwalls) show dulling of patterns, a tendency toward browns, and a generally eclipselike or henlike appearance. Either vermiculations are lost (Laysan Teal and Hawaiian Ducks) or some feathers of both vermiculated and barred types occur in the nuptial plumage (Kerguelen Pintails and presumably Washington Gadwalls). Females are even less patterned, showing a darker brown color in most cases and less marked individual feathers. The Hawaiian Duck and Laysan Teal differ in having feather patterns of high contrast. In northern anatids vermiculation and barring are known to be related to levels of the hormone testosterone (see Greij 1973 for review). Although similar hormone cycles must occur in southern anatids, the sensitivity to testosterone may have been altered by genetic selection against conspicuous patterns. A great opportunity exists for basic study of the physiology and genetics of plumage of island forms, but interpretation awaits work on common anatids of both hemispheres.

An observation of uncertain significance is that yearling Hawaiian Ducks tend to have showier (Mallard-like) plumages than older adults (Swedberg 1967). The mechanism and degree of this change are uncertain but may explain concern over variability of plumages noted by Rothschild (1893) and Perkins (1903). The relationship of the age-related change to variation in the Mariana Mallard has not been explored

Endemic island forms arising from southern anatids (South Georgia Pintails) appear little changed because they are derived from forms that either never had patterned feathers or have already lost them, and there appears to be no selection toward dichromatism. The lack of pattern change certainly influences the taxonomic interpretation and provides no measure of the time involved. Quite possibly the South Georgia Pintail originating from a dull-colored form has been isolated longer than the Kerguelen Pintail that originated from a bright form.

The situation with the Brown Teal complex is less clear-cut, since the patterns are obscure in both Brown Teal and Auckland Flightless Teal. Certainly significant in Auckland Flightless Teal is the loss of a wing speculum, which is no longer a display feature in a nonflying bird, and the fact that vermiculations in males are conspicuous on Brown Teal and Auckland Flightless Teal (Falla and Stead 1938).

It is difficult to identify the important influences on the generally dark coloration of island ducks. Camouflage certainly is an important character for a more terrestrial species, and the color of subantarctic and cold-temperate species blends well with the dark peat soils of tussock areas. Even the tropical island forms are typically dark. This may not be surprising in the Hawaiian Duck of a humid forested area, but Laysan Teal seem to be dark in spite of the light-colored sands of a quite different habitat.

Colors of the soft parts, particularly the bill, also may be duller in island ducks. This presumably is related to plumage dimorphism and camouflage. Galapagos Pintails have less red and hence less contrast in their bills. Laysan Teal and Hawaiian Ducks retain the general sexual differences in bill color, but the colors are less brilliant. Kerguelen Pintails retain a vivid blue and black bill similar to that of northern Pintails.

White Eye-rings

Whereas eye-rings are rare in other ducks, several endemic island forms have white eye-rings: Auckland Flightless Teal (Fig. 3.2) Brown Teal, Laysan Teal, Andaman Teal, Steamer Ducks, and a high percentage of Hawaiian Ducks. This occurrence seems more than coincidence. The single outstanding behavioral trait in at least four forms that have this character is that they actively feed at night, and three feed on terrestrial invertebrates. Many ducks feed at night, often in response to human activities (Thornberg 1973), and ducklings may do so regularly to take advantage of invertebrate behavior patterns (Swanson and Nelson 1970). But feeding of island ducks at night may be forced by the diel rhythm of food availability or by predators and seems to constitute a major portion of the feeding activity of several island ducks. Laysan Teal may take up to 95 percent of their food at night (Warner 1963), Brown Teal feed in uplands either by night or day (Weller 1974), Auckland Flightless Teal appear to be active on the forest floor at any time of day or night (Weller 1975a), and Andaman Teal feed in paddy fields at night (Butler 1896, Baker 1899); but terrestrial nocturnal feeding has not been established. The Andaman Teal is the only one of the four in which ducklings also have light eye-rings.

Hawaiian Ducks have been reported as feeding in the uplands (Munro 1944), but the incidence of nocturnal feeding is unknown. In those individuals in which an eye-ring occurs, seasonal variation in its size was noted by Swedberg (1967).

It is difficult to imagine any optical advantage to ducks in dim light, but white eye-rings may provide important visual signals between members of a feeding pair or family. Hailman (1977) indicates that eye contact is important in birds and that dark-headed birds often have light eye-rings that facilitate location of the eye. Four other ducks with white eye-rings happen to be hole-nesting species: the female North American Wood Duck (*Aix sponsa*), Mandarin Duck (*Aix galericulata*), Pink-eared Duck (*Malacorhynchus membranaceus*), and Black-bellied Whistling Duck (*Dendrocygna autumnalis*); but hole-nesting is not characteristic of any of the island ducks except possibly the Andaman Teal (Osmaston 1906). Wood Ducks and Whistling Ducks are known to be crepuscular or even nocturnal feeders, and the facial patterns may be important visual signals to mates or ducklings in the dim light of nest holes. Old Squaws however, have white eye-rings, and they nest on the ground; other species like Hooded Mergansers nest in holes and do not have eye-rings.

These speculations obviously can only be resolved by serious quantitation of nocturnal activities of ducks. Genetic studies might also be helpful, however, because the presumed inbreeding of small and isolated populations may be involved in the albinistic tendencies on the heads of Laysan and Andaman teal, which develop to extreme in captivity (Wright and Dewar 1925, Delacour 1956, Warner 1963).

Body Size

The comparisons made by Lack (1970) using mostly weight data from Lack (1968) and measurements from Delacour (1954, 1956, 1959)

TABLE 3.3

Mean body weights in grams of three island ducks compared to mainland counterparts, with estimated percentage decrease in size of island form (sample size in parentheses)

Form	Males		Females		Percent decreases	
	Continental	Island	Continental	Island	Male	Female
Mallard vs. Laysan Teal	1224(4091)*	502(2)†	1044(3277)*	488(2)†		
	…		…	450(1)‖		
	…	404(3)§	…	355(2)§		
Means	1224(4091)	463(5)	1044(3277)	427(5)	62.2	59.1
Mallard vs. Hawaiian Duck	1224(4091)*	668(16)#	1044(3277)*	572(7)#		
	…	658(12)**	…	593(12)**		
Means	1224(4091)	644(28)	1044(3277)	585(19)	45.8	44.0
Brown Teal vs. Flightless Teal	665(8)††§§	501(3)‖‖	630(10)††	380(4)‖		
	…	547(3)**	600(12)§§	…		
Means	665(8)	523(6)	614(22)	380(4)	21.4	38.1

*Bauer and von Blotzheim 1968.
†Specimens measured by J. Kear and Weller at Wildfowl Trust.
§Specimens at Univ. Calif. (Berkeley).
‖Lack 1968.
#Swedberg 1967.
**Weller unpubl.
††Gravatt 1966.
§§Reid and Roderick 1973.
‖J. Kear (pers. commun.).

document the reduction in size of island ducks. Weight changes were given only for females, however, and ranged from reductions of about one-half in Laysan Teal versus its Mallard ancestor, to two-thirds in South Georgia Pintails versus Brown Pintails. Additional data on weights of both sexes gathered on South Georgia Pintails (Weller 1975c) and Auckland Flightless Teal (Weller 1975d) are in general agreement with these patterns. Selected weight data presented in Table 3.3 show the reduction in size of three island species compared with their ancestral forms.

The difference in percent reduction in the weight of male Laysan Teal (62 percent) compared to Koloas (21 percent) may reflect time of isolation of the forms or possibly differences in archipelago size or habitat, since both reside in the same tropical latitude. Weight differences between Mallards and island derivatives far exceed differences between Brown Teal and Auckland Flightless Teal, presumably because the Brown Teal itself is an island form of reduced size.

With the exception of the nonmigratory Greenland Mallard (*Anas platyrhynchos conboschas*), which exceeds the continental Mallard in size, it is remarkable that the body size of most island forms that have been weighed, regardless of latitude or vegetation, are so similar in weight—all being about 400 g to 600 g (Lack 1970). The significance of this pattern from the standpoint of bioenergetics and food relationships is not clear, but it is a topic of considerable physiological and ecological importance. Data on other species are needed. Hundreds of Galapagos Pintails have been collected but few have been weighed, or at least such data have not been published. Two specimens in the Museum of Zoology at the University of California (Berkeley) fall within the usual island size range: a male of 425 g and a female of 450 g. Both Meller's Duck and the Philippine Duck seem to be large for island ducks, but weight data are not available.

Although sample size is very small, it is worth noting that weight of flightless ducks differs. The solely marine forms such as Steamer Ducks (two species) weigh from 2000 g to 6300 g, whereas Auckland Flightless Teal weigh less than 630 g. This size difference presumably is related to the rough waters and deep-diving habits of the steamer ducks.

A large series of measurements of island ducks of subantarctic areas has been tested statistically, and data on means, standard errors, and tests of significance are shown in Table 3.4. They confirm Lack's (1970) observations on some forms but also demonstrate previously unreported differences in Crozet and Kerguelen pintail populations.

TABLE 3.4

Differences in some measurements (in mm) of some endemic island ducks and their continental ancestors

Anas georgica georgica

	Drake				Hen				t-test between sexes
	No.	Mean	S.E.	t-test with A. g. spinicauda	No.	Mean	S.E.	t-test with A. g. spinicauda	
Culmen	21	34.7	0.29	17.30*	17	32.4	0.26	17.26*	4.57†
Tarsus	21	36.9	0.40	6.38*	17	36.1	0.29	4.70*	1.55
Tail	20	103.7	2.10	4.54*	17	89.8	1.72	0.49	5.01†
Wing	21	214.8	1.26	9.61*	17	204.1	1.39	8.94*	5.70†
Tail no.	19	16.0	0.0	145.10*	13	15.9	0.002	33.02*	48.70†
Anas g. spinicauda									
Culmen	19	44.4	0.50	...	10	41.2	0.50	...	3.84*
Tarsus	14	41.0	0.51	...	5	39.2	0.73	...	1.87
Tail	18	116.6	1.87	...	10	91.1	1.87	...	8.86*
Wing	17	234.9	1.68	...	10	223.0	1.41	...	4.85*
Tail no.	12	15.5	0.003	...	9	16.0	0.0	...	138.20*

TABLE 3.4. (continued)

Anas a. acuta

	Drake				Hen				
	No.	Mean	S.E.	t-test with A. a. eatoni	No.	Mean	S.E.	t-test with A. a. eatoni	t-test between sexes
Culmen	12	51.9	0.47	32.10*	7	46.2	0.63	26.68*	7.30*
Tarsus	12	42.8	0.47	17.50*	7	39.5	0.50	9.49*	4.42*
Tail	12	164.3	8.73	7.00*	7	100.3	3.07	5.29*	5.43*
Wing	12	261.8	1.06	20.13*	7	244.3	3.48	11.72*	5.92*
Tail no.	11	16.0	0.0	...	4	15.8	0.001	1.46	467.70*

Anas a. eatoni

	Drake				Hen				
	No.	Mean	S.E.	t-test with A. a. drygalski	No.	Mean	S.E.	t-test with A. a. drygalski	t-test between sexes
Culmen	19	33.7	0.34	1.67	9	31.0	0.13	2.06	5.33*
Tarsus	19	35.1	0.19	4.17*	9	32.5	0.49	2.39†	6.02*
Tail	19	105.2	3.87	0.95	9	85.2	0.86	2.00	3.50*
Wing	20	233.6	1.32	5.62*	9	203.4	1.50	0.55	9.15*
Tail no.	14	16.0	0.0	77.95*	7	15.1	0.404	1.60	3.16*

TABLE 3.4 (continued)

Anas a. drygalski

| | Drake | | | | Hen | | | | |
	No.	Mean	S.E.	t-test with A. a. acuta	No.	Mean	S.E.	t-test with A. a. acuta	t-test between sexes
Culmen	18	34.5	0.34	30.75*	5	31.8	0.48	16.86*	3.99*
Tarsus	18	36.4	0.25	12.20*	5	34.2	0.34	7.39*	4.31*
Tail	9	99.8	1.36	6.32*	5	81.2	2.24	4.63*	7.56*
Wing	17	212.0	1.61	23.50*	5	202.2	1.02	9.88*	3.20*
Tail no.	13	16.15	0.002	68.75*	4	16.0	0.0	250.00*	40.67*

Anas a. aucklandica

| | Drake | | | | Hen | | | | |
	No.	Mean	S.E.	t-test with A. a. chlorotis	No.	Mean	S.E.	t-test with A. a. chlorotis	t-test between sexes
Culmen	16	39.45	0.27	8.90*	5	36.2	0.48	3.33*	5.67*
Tarsus	13	35.1	0.39	8.30*	3	32.3	0.33	4.46*	3.10†
Tail	16	81.6	2.14	3.29*	5	61.2	0.97	9.57*	4.91*
Wing	16	137.5	1.09	35.30*	5	126.4	2.04	27.96*	4.76*
Tail no.	6	17.0	0.45	...	2	17.0	1.0	0.58	...

Anas anas chlorotis

| | Drake | | | | Hen | | | | |
	No.	Mean	S.E.		No.	Mean	S.E.		t-test between sexes
Culmen	18	42.7	0.27	...	13	39.1	0.50	...	6.80*
Tarsus	15	40.7	0.55	...	11	37.5	0.58	...	3.93*
Tail	19	90.2	1.54	...	14	83.7	1.34	...	3.05*
Wing	19	198.3	1.32	...	12	188.1	1.15	...	5.37*
Tail no.	1	14.0	...	...	5	15.6	...	...	...

*Significant at (P < 0.01)
†Significant at (P < 0.05)

Speciation on Islands

The more distinctive forms emphasized in this treatment presumably represent cases of longer or more complete isolation on islands or populations that for some reason have varied more rapidly. In some if not most cases reproductive isolation probably has been reached, but this cannot be tested effectively because of the propensity of waterfowl for hybridization in captivity (Johnsgard 1960). Their taxonomic classification then becomes debatable. Other examples in birds have been summarized by Mayr (1965).

In trying to explain the large number of endemic island birds, Miller (1966) suggested that few island species successfully expand their ranges to include adjacent continents. Their genetic systems are products of selection against the mobility and high reproductive rate necessary to pioneering. Insular species are, however, better adapted to pioneering on other islands (Salomonsen 1976). Ricklefs and Cox (1972) have theorized that many endemics are the end product of a series of evolutionary stages that range from expanding or widespread species to the restricted ones that eventually are represented only as endemics.

There are numerous examples in ducks where continental species have nonmigratory subspecies on nearby islands. In the case of the Greenland Mallard, the subspecies is recognizable only by its larger body size and slight color differences (Delacour 1956). Other ducks that probably were influenced by island subspeciation are the Gray Teal, Gray Duck, Radjah Shelduck (*Tadorna radjah*) and Cotton Pygmy Goose (*Nettapus cormandelianus*) in Australasia, all of which have recognizable subspecies influenced by isolation on New Guinea or some other island where there is little interchange among populations. Several migratory Arctic island geese are probably island isolates (Table 1.3), and others were discussed by Lack (1974).

In most cases the evolutionary history of island species is impossible to trace, but several examples are worth noting. The Cuban or Black-billed Whistling Duck is widespread on a series of islands. Presumably it evolved on a larger island such as Cuba and gradually spread to other islands similar in habitat and lacking in real competitors. At least at present no comparable habitat exists in the United States to which it could have spread. A superficially similar relative halfway around the world is the Spotted Whistling Duck, prevalent in New Guinea and islands west to the southern Philippines and east to the Bismark Archipelago. It presumably had a still wider range of islands to pioneer than did the Cuban Whistling Duck and could successfully compete, but it has not reached the Solomon Islands to the southeast or Borneo to the west.

The Ruddy-headed Sheldgoose (*Chloëphaga rubidiceps*) breeds on the Falkland Islands, Tierra del Fuego, and a restricted area in Chilean

Patagonia. The population in the Falkland Islands seems to be sedentary, but the Tierra del Fuego population migrates to southern Buenos Aires province of Argentina in winter (Olrog 1963). Ecological isolation of this small monochromatic form from the Upland Sheldgoose (*C. picta*) is uncertain, but it frequents drier regions in Tierra del Fuego. Whether it evolved on the Falkland Islands (which would seem like a better isolating site) or on Tierra del Fuego, it may be an island species that has expanded to one island or the other across some 300 km of water.

CHAPTER 4

Development of Island Faunas

Mᴜᴄʜ of the previous discussion has centered about unique and sometimes solitary island species. Such species demonstrate considerable adaptation to island living, especially in food selection and feeding behavior. But these forms differ mainly in size, color, and terrestrial behavior as opposed to the major morphological adaptations for diverse niches that have occurred in the radiation of Galapagos finches (subfamily Geospizinae), Hawaiian honeycreepers (family Drepanididae), and similar groups (Lack 1947, Amadon 1966, Miller 1966). This may be a result of time, niche diversity, and limitations of the basic model we call a duck.

Species complexes of waterfowl, on islands or on continents, probably have arisen more by the dispersal and adjustments of species into an established fauna than by speciation in the area. It is apparent from several studies that additions and deletions are common in island faunas and turnover rates of species are higher for island faunas than for continental ones (Salomonsen 1976). The rate of turnover and the calculated extinction rates for island birds are much debated (Lynch and Johnson 1974, Jones and Diamond 1976, Salomonsen 1976), and the small number of ducks involved makes meaningful calculations improbable. What happens to the original species with each new arrival, and what competition does the new species face? By relating niche segregation of various anatids to available habitats on islands with few to many species, we get some idea of the types of adaptation to the competitive situation in which subsequent colonizers are placed. Unfortunately, this can only be done in qualitative terms.

The apparent ecological expansion or release of several endemic and solitary island anatids was discussed earlier. For comparison let us now consider the "two-duck island," "three-duck island," etc., to appraise how newly added species may "squeeze" into the system. This process of adjustment is called "species packing" or "ecological contraction" (MacArthur and Wilson 1967) and results in reduced habitat use and,

TABLE 4.1
Ducks of the Auckland Islands

REGULAR BREEDERS
  Auckland Flightless Teal (*Anas a. aucklandica*)
  Gray Duck (*A. superciliosa*)
  Mallard (*A. platyrhynchos*)

ACCIDENTALS
  New Zealand Shoveler (*A. rhynchotis variegata*)

EXTINCT
  Auckland Merganser (*Mergus australis*)

Note: After Falla et al. (1967) and Weller (1975d).

with time, probably reduced niche breadth. South Georgia can serve as the initial stage of an island with 2 species; the Auckland Islands had 3 species (Table 4.1) with some recent shifts; New Zealand had 7, and 4 have been successfully introduced (Table 2.3); the Falkland Islands have 11, and at least 4 more occur sporadically (Table 2.2); and Tierra del Fuego has 16 or more (Table 2.1), essentially the complement of sizable continental areas.

Competition for food resources is one of the major considerations in understanding how many species can share an area and its resources. Reduction in competition may involve use of different habitats, different feeding strategies and foods, different food sizes, and seasonal variation in habitat or food use.

Division of resources by habitat is common in larger taxonomic groups (tribes or genera) such as geese grazing in the uplands, sea ducks diving along the coast, or dabbling ducks filter-feeding in very shallow wetlands. However, such gross habitat classifications do not reflect all the potential feeding sites; and the use of different water depths, vegetative zones (Weller 1972, White and James 1978), and food sizes and types (Stott and Olson 1973) as well as feeding behavior may reduce competition.

Feeding specializations of anatids include herbivores, omnivores, and carnivores. Swans, geese, sheldgeese, and wigeons use grasses, sedges, and aquatic succulents. Omnivores such as dabblers and pochards use invertebrates of various types and sizes (especially prior to and during the breeding or rearing periods) plus seeds and foliage of aquatic plants (especially during the nonbreeding period). Carnivores such as sea ducks favor invertebrates or vertebrates and utilize little or no plant food.

Segregation of food use by specialization of bill shape or body size to enhance the taking of different-sized foods is common among birds (Diamond 1972, Cody 1974) and is obvious in ducks (mergansers versus dabbling ducks, for example). Another means of reducing competition for foods is the use of the same habitat by different species at different times of the year, an unlikely arrangement in water areas of high latitudes because of winter freeze-up.

It is difficult to appraise the maximum number of niches available on these islands and whether all the niches are full. Additionally, we face several major problems in ecology: how much overlap can exist among species, and how much does the narrow niche resulting from ecological contraction influence population size?

One estimate of niche suitability for waterfowl is assessment of the niches that exist in the most complex faunas of large and complex land masses. But this is a complicated situation because of the large number of species involved and the fact that several species seem to use the same foods. Thus it may be easier to identify the segregating mechanisms in simpler island groupings. It would be ideal if we could experimentally add species at will or have numerous replicates of island sizes and species complexes as did Simberloff (1976) working with insects, but this is not possible with waterfowl.

South Georgia

South Georgia once had one species and now has two; is there room for three?

In the immature, climatically limited environment of South Georgia, one adaptable duck has survived in reasonable numbers by its ecological expansion to all habitats (tussock grass, stream, pond, and seashore) (Fig. 4.1) and a variety of food types (filamentous and leafy marine algae; terrestrial, freshwater, and marine invertebrates of various sizes; and even carrion). No other species of duck was known to nest on the island, although other species certainly must have reached there since the establishment of the pintail. South Georgia once was glaciated to the sea but now has a narrow ring of tussock grass, freshwater basins that act as nutrient sumps, and a temperate regime that permits survival of hardy ducklings over the winter. If the climate continues to ameliorate, the glaciers will recede further, and other plants and invertebrates will increase community diversity, presumably increase community stability, and produce further food resources that ducks may use.

We were fortunate to witness breeding of the second pioneering species, the Speckled Teal (Weller and Howard 1972). Food for waterfowl is sparse except in the ponds in summer, which must be a seasonal burst as it is at Signy Island (Heywood 1967), or on the seashore. These two duck species may compete to a point of extinction of one (this interaction contributes to the commonness of island extinctions), or they must use food resources in such a way that major competition is avoided. It is logical to assume that the form that is present sufficiently long to have gained morphological distinctiveness (in this case, the South Georgia Pintail) has a competitive advantage. But the second recorded pioneer is also a well-adapted, successful, and widespread species sympatric with the ancestral form of the South Georgia Pintail (the Brown Pintail) in South America. Perhaps this is usually the case. Remotely, they may have resolved some of the competitive interaction prior to colonization of South Georgia. Hybridization also is no problem, as reproductive isolation is virtually complete (Johnsgard 1960).

Although I have collected only five South Georgia Pintails and one Speckled Teal, observations of their feeding behavior strongly support the limited food habits data. These observations suggest that adult pintails and teal use some of the same foods. However, Speckled Teal probably feed in summer more on small crustaceans (like *Daphnia* and *Cyclops*) on the surface and perhaps in shallower waters and mud flats than do South Georgia Pintails, which use larger food items (like fairy shrimp) from benthic sites or deeper water. Availability of nest sites should be adequate, but the young undoubtedly will be reared on the warmer protected ponds as opposed to the cold and often hazardous fjords. Competition of young may be more serious, and this new two-species complex deserves special observation in the next few years.

The Speckled Teal seems preadapted for life with the South Georgia Pintail; no other species from the Falkland Islands complement would have fit more efficiently. However, this does not mean that one species may influence populations of the other. I suspect that, based on its morphological adaptations, the South Georgia Pintail is utilizing the food resources optimally, and that population expansion is unlikely. If the Speckled Teal uses essentially the same resources, will the total number of ducks (or total kilograms of ducks) remain unchanged but be divided between two species rather than concentrated in one? Or will the feeding of the smaller Speckled Teal more efficiently exploit a resource less well used by South Georgia Pintails, so that total duck biomass will increase? The latter presumably must occur, or species richness would tend to remain stable rather than increase.

Our knowledge of waterfowl makes it difficult to assess accurately what species will be the third pioneer. Species preadapted by island living on the Falkland Islands may be logically scanned for possible pioneers, so it will be best to consider that island complex before attempting predictions.

Auckland Islands

The Auckland Islands once had three species, then had two, and now has three again. Is there room for four?

84

Fig. 4.1. Typical South Georgia Pintail habitat including freshwater ponds (left), and Moraine Fjord (right) at Dartmouth Point, South Georgia.

The bioclimatic situation of the Auckland Islands is drastically different from South Georgia. Truly an oceanic, cold-temperate island rather than a subantarctic one (except perhaps at high altitudes), it is high, well drained, unglaciated, and relatively mild in climate. These islands are extensively forested except in areas of salt spray, in soggy tussock drainages, or at high altitudes or other areas exposed to the strong winds. One is primarily impressed with the absence of the rich freshwater wetlands most people associate with waterfowl. Instead, the habitat is dominated by brown-colored and sterile-looking streams, minimal estuarine habitat, moist and dense forest and scrub, and rugged seashore. One quickly concludes that any duck living there must use

either the streams or the seashore because tussock-rimmed puddles and ponds are rare. Habitat segregation by the three ducks that once occurred probably was not quite that simple, but the division is fairly logical.

Prior to 1902 three species involving two endemics occurred on these islands: the Auckland Merganser, last seen in 1902 (Kear and Scarlett 1970); the Auckland Flightless Teal that I was able to study in 1972; and the Gray Duck, which probably has never occurred in large numbers (Table 2.4). The Mallard has recently pioneered from New Zealand, is increasing in numbers, and seems to be hybridizing with Gray Ducks there as elsewhere.

The excellent review of the Auckland Merganser by Kear and Scarlett (1970) has demonstrated that it was a stream species that apparently fed mostly on fish (*Gallaxias brevipennis*). It was occasionally seen in estuaries and harbors, but its specialization clearly seems to have been that of a stream carnivore. There is no evidence that the species survives anywhere. Falla reported that it was not seen during World War II despite much searching (Falla et al. 1967) and G. R. Williams and I searched for it on Adams Island and the south part of the main Auckland Island in 1972 and found no sign of it (Williams and Weller 1974). If present, which seems very unlikely, it is indeed rare.

Little is known of the Gray Duck except that it is widespread but low in number. Nests and broods have been observed along wooded streams and in tussock-rimmed pools, but it is nowhere abundant. Pairs and flocks use estuaries and the larger rivers near sea level. Mallards probably will overlap in food selection, but I noted Mallards using tidal pools and even feeding in debris collected in marine coves. Because of the usual food habits of dabbling ducks, it is doubtful that Gray Ducks were in any way competitive with Auckland Mergansers.

The truly dominant duck on the Aucklands is the Flightless Teal. At one time it seems to have occurred on the shorelines and grassy areas of all the islands. There have been few or no reports of it on the main island since pigs and cats have become widespread, but the ruggedness of the shorelines may limit their use for feeding as well. The species has expanded to virtually every possible niche except streams, so it too was an unlikely competitor with the Auckland Merganser. Surprisingly, Auckland Flightless Teal still do not use streams after an apparent absence of mergansers for 70 years.

My own experience with the Auckland Flightless Teal is dominated by observation of a population dependent upon the sea. Other members of the 1972–73 Auckland Islands expedition found teal in boggy tussock fields at 210 m to 240 m elevation on Disappointment Island, and we saw much use of grasses and forbs on all the islands. Nevertheless, one is left with the impression that the species could never have survived on the basis of freshwater areas on the islands. Moreover, it is probably this scarcity of wetlands that limits Gray Ducks and may limit Mallards as well. Teal are well adapted to the seashore and the littoral zone. As on most southern high-latitude islands, the seashore is the richest area for exploitation, and apparently no oceanic birds can forage as efficiently as a duck. Auckland Flightless Teal feed on a variety of invertebrates of various sizes taken by probing in wind-rowed kelp, dabbling in rock algae at low tide, or diving in shallow waters. They feed in soft soil and on carrion and are highly terrestrial at night or day. They reflect long adaptation to these islands in a way that prevents either the Gray Duck or Mallard from becoming a serious competitor.

Is there a vacant niche for another anatid on the Auckland Islands? Probably the New Zealand Brown Teal could survive in estuarine areas, but such areas are not extensive. Blue Mountain Ducks might survive in the streams, but the invertebrate populations are probably limited in these acid waters. Falla et al. (1967) indicated that shovelers had been recorded on the island, but there is little habitat to maintain a viable population. Hence, it is probable that ducks are exploiting the available habitat of the island and species richness here is habitat limited.

New Zealand

New Zealand has seven native species and four introduced species as well.

Because of its size, New Zealand is perhaps more continent than island; but its isolation from Australia, by 1920 km and differences in habitat, and from the tropical islands, which are a poor source area for waterfowl, may have reduced species richness there. It is particularly difficult to appraise the diversity of habitats in this relatively small area, but topographic and climatic diversity are well known. Lentic habitats are fairly common and diverse. Wetlands vary from large and sterile mountain lakes to naturally heated lakes to extensive marsh areas. In addition, there are numerous artificial reservoirs and wetlands.

Five of the seven native species (Table 2.3) are endemic and ecologically isolated. The small and torrential streams are used by Blue Mountain Ducks that feed on stream invertebrates in a habitat rarely used by other ducks (Kear and Steel 1971). Only the Andean Torrent Duck equals or exceeds adaptation of the Blue Mountain Duck to torrential streams.

The New Zealand Scaup, whose ancestor may be the northern Tufted Duck (Hutton 1871), is the only open-lake and marsh anatid. It nests in emergent vegetation (Oliver 1955) and probably feeds on aquatic vegetation and associated snails and other invertebrates.

The New Zealand or Paradise Shelduck is a grazer associated with meadows of larger stream valleys. It is widely distributed and is spreading due to agricultural activities such as pasture development and stock-pond construction (McAllum 1965).

The Brown Teal is now mainly an estuarine species utilizing invertebrate foods. However, it supposedly was once widespread in marshes and slow-moving streams near the sea. The extent of its ecological isolation with other members of the genus *Anas* is unknown, but its major habitat may always have been estuaries.

New Zealand Shovelers differ only subspecifically from the Australian form (*Anas r. rhynchotis*). Presumably, they have not been isolated long or there is regular infusion of Australian stock, as suggested by Sibson (1967). Like other shovelers, this is a planktonic strainer well adapted to open marshes and rich, shallow pools. Because the bill and lamellae of Brown Teal seem adapted to straining out invertebrates, it may be that shovelers are relatively recent arrivals to the fauna; and because they are still better adapted as strainer-feeders, they may have influenced habitat use by Brown Teal. The Brown Teal mainly uses estuaries, which are vulnerable habitats in the development of a growing nation, and it is now on the endangered species list.

Gray Teal appear to be relatively recent arrivals from Australia (Fleming 1962) and they are associated with small or shallow muddy wetlands. Their ecological isolation from Gray Ducks has not been studied, but most anatid complexes are characterized by both large and small varieties that use similar plant and invertebrate food types but differ in sizes of foods taken due to bill and lammellae size. Gray Ducks are common and widespread and use a great variety of habitats from marshes to streams (Balham 1952, Oliver 1955). They are Mallard-like, have diverse food habits, and seem to be the most numerous and widespread species of duck in New Zealand.

Perhaps the most fascinating aspect of New Zealand waterfowl is the large-scale experiment in niche availability that has been conducted there. New Zealand has been the classic example of multiple introductions of exotics because of the depauperate fauna (Wodzicki 1965). Introductions were justified for various social reasons including efforts to make a greater harvest of wildfowl available for hunting. The assumption has been that niches are available and vacant as a result of New Zealand's isolation. An "experiment" of this scale is worthy of consideration in view of Lack's (1970) argument that island faunas are habitat limited rather than limited by the ability of pioneers to reach the land mass.

Successful introductions in New Zealand include Mallards, which are so similar to Gray Ducks that they probably use the same niche. The Mallard is more productive and less mobile and seems to be out-producing the Gray Duck (Balham and Miers 1959) as well as hybridizing with it (Williams 1970, Williams and Roderick 1973). The Giant Canada Goose (*Branta canadensis maxima*) has been very successful in establishing itself and adapting to use of large river systems (as this race originally did in the United States) and agricultural crops. They are regarded as pests and often are not protected even though they serve as game species (Imber and Williams 1968). Black Swans (*Cygnus atratus*) introduced from Australia have adapted so successfully that they have spread and nest in extremely dense colonies such as at Lake Ellesmere. Mute Swans

(*Cygnus olor*) are much less successful but are widespread in small populations.

The Cape Barren Goose (*Cereopsis novae-hollandiae*) was introduced from Australia and Tasmania, but stocked populations failed. Recent natural pioneers from Australia (Williams 1968) have arrived on the southwestern coasts of the South Island but have not become established.

Fleming (1962) estimated that seven species of birds had been added to the New Zealand avifauna in the past century. Other natural introductions from Australia were briefly successful and then died out, as in the case of the Australian White-eye. The Plumed Whistling Duck (*Dendrocygna eytoni*) and Maned Goose (*Chenonetta jubata*) also have been seen occasionally (Purdue 1871, Ornith. Soc. New Zealand 1953), and the Australian Pink-eared Duck and Musk Duck (*Biziura lofata*) are known from recent fossil remains (Falla 1953, Williams 1962). The Auckland Merganser presumably had a long history of differentiation in New Zealand and was found in Maori middens but was extinct by the time of white settlers' arrival; it survived only on the Auckland Islands (Kear and Scarlett 1970).

Thus the history of natural and intentional introduction suggests that unfilled niches did exist. Certainly some of these niches may be new, man-made habitats such as those used by the Canada Goose and New Zealand Shelduck. Sibson (1967) suggested that increases in shovelers were due to reservoirs and sewage lagoons. But successful introductions like the Black Swan were presumably due to use of natural habitats. Moreover, either the same swan or another subrecent species apparently occurred in New Zealand when the Maoris arrived and thereafter was extirpated for unknown reasons (Howard 1975, Kear and Murton 1976).

Falkland Islands

The Falkland Islands have eleven breeding species and several visitors.

Considering islands or archipelagoes only by the number of species present is misleading in some ways, but perhaps it makes obvious other influential factors such as distance from source and similarity of habitats that influence pioneering potential. Thus on a considerably smaller total land mass than New Zealand, the Falkland Islands have 11 regular breeders (see Table 2.2) of various abundance levels and some accidentals that nest periodically.

Distance clearly is a minor problem in reaching the Falkland

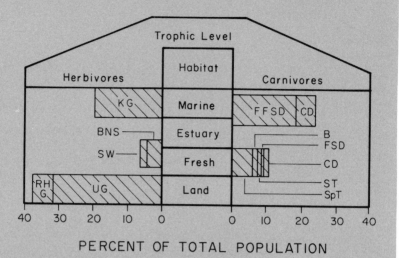

Fig. 4.2. Population distribution of Falkland waterfowl arranged by trophic level and habitat. (KG = Kelp Sheldgoose, BNS = Black-necked Swan, SW = Southern Wigeon, RHG = Ruddy-headed Sheldgoose, UG = Upland Sheldgoose, FFSD = Falkland Flightless Steamer Duck, CD = Crested Duck, B = Brown Pintail, FSD = Flying Steamer Duck, ST = Silver Teal, SpT = Speckled Teal.)

Islands, and the utilization of niches is strongly influenced by the similarity in habitat between the Falkland Islands and Tierra del Fuego. Many South American species are essentially preadapted for the Falkland Islands because of similar vegetative and climatic conditions that produce a similar number of potential niches.

The climatic regime in the Falkland Islands is demonstrated by monthly temperature means (Fig. 2.5) and adequate rainfall varying from about 550 mm in the west to 875 mm in the east. High winds, periodicity of rainfall, and character of the soils make growth of trees impossible; the result is a grassland made up of a few dominants. Varied wetlands are interspersed mostly at lower elevations (Weller 1972). Reduced productivity is a feature of the cold and acid water, however, and it is not surprising to find that the dominant species are those that use the extensive grassland or the coastal areas. The major habitat niches and their relative use for feeding are shown in Figure 4.2. During this study, nearly 40 percent of all waterfowl seen were terrestrial grazers, constituting an even larger share of the total biomass.

The 11 established species segregate by the four major habitats: grasslands, coastal areas, ponds and lakes, and streams. Within each, food specialization seems to prevent competition, but there are some unresolved problems.

Ruddy-headed Sheldgeese and Falkland Upland Sheldgeese share the terrestrial grasslands, but the manner in which they are segregated to avoid competition is uncertain. Ruddy-headed Sheldgeese tend to be in the western, drier parts of the Falkland Islands and the northern dry grasslands of Tierra del Fuego. However, Falkland Upland Sheldgeese are present in both areas, and they feed on short, green meadow grasses. Ruddy-headed Sheldgeese may tolerate coarser grasses and drier sites.

The seashore is used mainly by Falkland Flightless Steamer Ducks, which are efficient divers utilizing littoral benthos. Crested Ducks mostly use estuaries or protected coves, where they feed on invertebrates in moist or flooded gravel and algae. It is possible that young of the two species may compete for a short period; but young Falkland Flightless Steamer Ducks start diving for food in open water soon after they are dry, whereas Crested Ducks usually forage along the shore. Selection of different food sizes and habitat and feeding methods segregate these two species most of the time. The coastal marine herbivore is the Falkland Kelp Sheldgoose (Figs. 3.3 and 4.3), but Black-necked Swans and Southern Wigeons probably use some coastal plant resources as well.

The streams are used mainly by Speckled Teal that take small food items, probably from the native waterweed *Myriophyllum elatinoides*. However, Southern Wigeons may take *Lileopsis* sp. in small streams, and larger tidal estuaries that contain *Ruppia* sp. are favored by Southern Wigeons and Black-necked Swans. All three of these species also use ponds and lakes more frequently during the breeding period.

Ponds and lakes are of diverse types, but few are truly productive unless the bottoms are sand or clay as opposed to peat (Weller 1972). These are suitable substrates for a variety of invertebrates and plants favored by waterfowl as food. A number of species feed together in these rich ponds or lakes as elsewhere, and this competition may have influenced how segregation occurs, when it does. There is certainly considerable overlap in diets, especially of the less common species.

The deepwater, benthic feeder is the Falkland Flying Steamer Duck, which is usually found in lakes where there are fingernail clams or snails. Brown Pintails do not dive regularly but can reach benthos because of their long necks.

Speckled Teal and Silver Teal (*Anas versicolor fretensis*) use shallower water; I believe they are segregated by the smaller (even microscopic) food items taken by Speckled Teal in soupy mud or at the surface in submergent plants. Silver Teal feed on the bottom while swimming, whereas Speckled Teal quite happily walk or swim to feed.

Are there presently unused niches in the Falkland Islands? Because of the distance involved, most South American species tolerant of this climatic regime probably have had a sufficient number of individuals

Fig. 4.3. Rock outcrops used by Kelp Sheldgeese for feeding and kelp beds near Fox Bay
East, West Falkland Island.

visit the Falkland Islands that colonization was possible if the food
resources and other habitat features were available. Speculation on why
other species have not become established in the Falkland Islands will
follow consideration of the anatids of Tierra del Fuego.

Tierra del Fuego

Tierra del Fuego has 16 species or more, with niches packed.
This area has more diverse habitats than the Falkland Islands
because of the Andes and associated mountains that form the western
and southern boundaries of Isla Grande. Snowmelt produces diverse
stream sizes, often torrential, and high moisture levels produce extensive

beech forests. These mountains also produce a rain "shadow" so that northeastern Tierra del Fuego is arid grassland similar to parts of Patagonia (see Humphrey et al. 1970 for additional data on vegetation and climate). Glaciated terrain has resulted in rolling topography and some large and rich marshes in the lowlands. As a result anatid diversity is greater than on the Falkland Islands; on the whole, floral and faunal diversity as well as productivity seem greater. However, there are no endemic species or subspecies; all overlap into Patagonia.

All 11 species that breed regularly on the Falkland Islands occur on Tierra del Fuego except that the Falkland Flightless Steamer Duck is considered specifically different from the Magellanic Flightless Steamer Duck of Tierra del Fuego. The Kelp Sheldgoose and Upland Sheldgoose are recognized as separate subspecies. In addition, at least 5 other species not found regularly on the Falkland Islands are regarded as resident

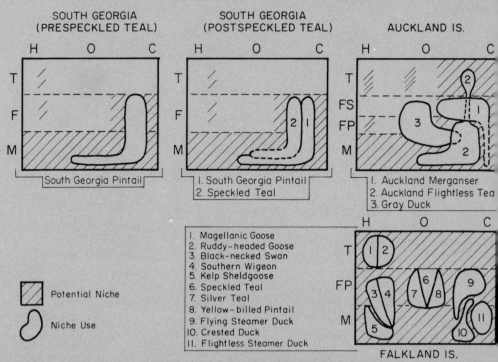

Fig. 4.4. Theoretical and observed patterns of habitat use of three subantarctic islands arranged by trophic level (H = herbivore, O = omnivore, C = carnivore) and habitat (T = terrestrial, F = freshwater, FP = freshwater pond, FS = freshwater stream, M = marine).

breeding birds in Tierra del Fuego: the Ashy-headed Sheldgoose (*Chloëphaga poliocephala*), Red Shoveler (*Anas platalea*), Coscoroba (*Coscoroba coscoroba*), Torrent Duck, and Bronze-winged Duck (*Anas specularis*). Moreover, Rosy-billed Pochards (*Netto peposaca*) have been seen in western Isla Grande by C. Olrog (pers. commun.) who believes they were breeding because of observed broody behavior of a female. However, my own observations suggest that most of these additional species and the Silver Teal (also rare to uncommon on the Falkland Islands) are in suboptimal habitats, except possibly the Red Shoveler.

Discussion

Based on general observation of the various possible food resources on several subantarctic islands, I have attempted to compare food availability and food use by various species in Figure 4.4. The assessment of habitats is speculative, and the breadth of the niches is estimated. Nevertheless, some dramatic differences occur that reflect maturity of the ecological systems, distance and size factors, and integration of non-competing species into the faunal complex. In most cases we know too little about the ecological requirements of individual species to quantitate why they are present or absent, but some considerations follow.

The series of islands of Tierra del Fuego, the Falklands, and South Georgia are especially interesting because of their size and spatial and species relationships. The largest complex is on Tierra del Fuego, with several species there not regular in the Falkland Islands. The reason these additional species occur on Tierra del Fuego and are absent in the Falkland Islands is worthy of speculation. The Ashy-headed Sheldgoose is a forest species (Johnson 1965), a habitat lacking in the Falkland Islands. Red Shovelers use plankton of rich semiopen waters; the shortage of nitrogen and phosphates in Falkland soils would rarely produce a sufficiently rich pond to maintain the macrofauna needed. Rapids are lacking or rare so that water and foods for torrent ducks are inadequate. Wooded lakes are nonexistent and slow-moving streams are rare; hence, Bronze-winged Ducks would find little habitat. Rosy-bills also use benthose-rich marshes for feeding and emergent plants for nesting—a type of habitat nonexistent in the Falkland Islands. Hence, it seems unlikely that other species from Tierra del Fuego will find conditions on the Falkland Islands suitable; neither area seems to have vacant niches that can support a viable population under present climatic conditions.

Reduced faunal diversity on South Georgia as compared to either Tierra del Fuego or the Falkland Islands is more clear-cut because productivity and habitat diversity are much reduced on South Georgia. The small pools or ponds are highly acid and produce only a few invertebrates in quantity. The seashore is probably the richest area, but the coastal plain is limited; only a few species of grasses and forbs are suitable for grazing. Moreover, the climate is more rigorous. Of the Falkland species, the Kelp Sheldgoose could find suitable foods on South Georgia, and it resides on equally rugged coastlines and in extensive tidal zones in the Falkland Islands and Tierra del Fuego but at less severe temperatures. The impact of this temperature regime on the young would be a crucial factor. Moreover, the Kelp Sheldgoose seems disinclined to fly, and 1200 km is a long distance in this latitude of turbulent winds.

The Southern Wigeon might be able to obtain sufficient marine vegetation to survive on South Georgia, but there are virtually no freshwater plant foods and these seem necessary for rearing its young.

The Falkland Upland Sheldgoose has been introduced to South Georgia twice (Watson 1975); both introductions failed, although the birds reproduced briefly (Matthews 1929). Presumably, an insufficient area of suitable grasses is free of snow during winter.

My best guess is that the ponds on South Georgia are too immature (of low productivity) to support marsh species that are not also adapted to using estuaries. The Brown Pintail, Speckled Teal, Southern Wigeon, and Crested Duck are the main users of such habitats on the Falklands. Of these only the Crested Duck truly uses seashores to rear its young. Moreover, the alpine race must tolerate quite severe temperatures. The Crested Duck could utilize fjord and marine-cove invertebrates, but these are now used intensively by South Georgia Pintails; thus competition would be a factor immediately, and this may explain why the Brown Pintail is not common on the Falkland Islands. Of all the species there, the Crested Duck may have the greatest pioneering potential for South Georgia, but this species has not been recorded to date. Isolation and climatic regimes probably have reduced the rate of waterfowl establishment there.

Among the islands considered here, only New Zealand seems to have had niches that were vacant and have been filled by successful natural and artificial introductions. New Zealand has the mildest climate and has varied habitats comparable to the much smaller Tierra del Fuego, but it seems that its isolation from similar habitats must have reduced the number and success of natural introductions. However, New Zealand waterfowl fauna has been adequate to saturate the Auckland Islands.

Conservation

ISLANDS have been a major stimulus for the development of evolutionary theory (initiated by Charles Darwin and Alfred Wallace), the maturation of modern concepts of systematics (Mayr 1965), and the development of biogeographic theory (MacArthur and Wilson 1967, Lack 1976). Currently, there is intensive research effort in all these areas, with rising recognition of the scientific value of islands and concern over the plight of island flora and fauna. However, there is considerable difference of opinion by scientists over what taxa are worthy of preservation, how this should be done, and how much money should be dedicated to the effort.

The loss of species seems to be a common population phenomenon characteristic of islands, with an equilibrium commonly established between gains from immigrants and natural losses (MacArthur and Wilson 1967). Although extinction is a natural process that has reoccurred many times throughout geologic history, man often has been the direct or indirect force that eliminated the balance essential to maintenance of these unique island forms. This is not surprising considering the uniqueness and adaptations of populations that like the Laysan Teal survive on a tiny island of less than 500 ha. Whether the Laysan Teal evolved on Laysan or whether this island is merely the last holdout of a species once widespread on Pacific islets, it was the introduction of rabbits by man that disturbed the delicate ecosystem (Warner 1963, Kear 1977).

Until recently it was assumed that the Auckland Merganser was endemic only to those islands, without considering the obvious probablility that New Zealand was the stepping-stone and perhaps the area of differentiation of the species. Kear and Scarlett (1970) have shown subfossil evidence of its more widespread distribution in New Zealand. The reason for its loss cannot be stated, for although collectors may have "cast the final stone," the species obviously was near natural extinction.

Tropical islands probably have suffered the greatest losses of natural features and species because so many have been inhabited permanently by man. At least two tropical island ducks now are extinct (the

Washington Gadwall and probably the Rennell Gray Teal), several have dangerously restricted numbers or distributions due to human activities (Mariana Mallard, Laysan Teal, Hawaiian Duck, Hawaiian Goose, Cuban Whistling Duck), and the Madagascar Teal is rare for unknown reasons.

Although most people think of subantarctic and cold-temperate islands as more pristine, they currently lack human inhabitants only after many unsuccessful attempts to settle and survive. Moreover, because many of these islands were on the great southern shipping route, mariners attempted to establish every form of domestic animal in event of a subsequent shipwreck. Whalers and sealers, who resided on islands even temporarily, also released food animals including mammals such as Reindeer (*Rangifer tarandus*). On South Georgia, reindeer have proven successful; they are destructive and are spreading. Reindeer also were introduced on Kerguelen Island (Prevost and Mougin 1970). Holdgate and Wace (1961) listed the numerous mammals introduced on southern islands.

Whereas livestock have acted mostly as modifiers of the vegetation, introduced cats, dogs, foxes, and pigs have been predators. One introduced predator, the mongoose, has been cited earlier as especially damaging to the Lesser Whistling Duck on Fiji and the Koloa and possibly the Nene on the Hawaiian Islands. The introduction of the Patagonia Fox (*Dusicyon griseus*) to Tierra del Fuego may be the cause of reduction of the Ruddy-headed Sheldgoose there (Weller 1975a). Introduced Arctic (*Alopex lagopus*) and Red (*Vulpes fulva*) foxes on the Aleutian Islands may have been responsible for the decline of the Aleutian Canada Goose (*Branta canadensis leucopareia*). Reintroduction of hand-reared birds was preceded by fox removal. Although the relative values of predator control and captive rearing cannot be assessed, the program is still being viewed positively. Brown Rats (*Rattus norvegicus*) have depleted populations of Antarctic Pipits (*Anthus antarcticus*) on the larger islands of South Georgia but have not eliminated the South Georgia Pintail. Mink (*Mustela vision*) were introduced on Kerguelen Island but, fortunately, were not successful (Prevost and Mougin 1970).

The introduction of more direct competitors may reduce native species because of the relatively low species richness or productivity on these islands, which minimizes available food resources. The competition for invertebrates by introduced trout and the Blue Mountain Duck in New Zealand is a potential problem of uncertain magnitude (Kear 1973). The Rennell Gray Teal now appears to be extinct, and it has been suggested that competition with the introduced fish *Tilapia* sp. may have been a major factor in its decline (Kear and Williams 1978).

The introduction of ducks (usually for sport hunting) is even more dangerous because of more direct competition for food and the greater reproductive potential of continental forms. Mallards have been extremely successful in New Zealand, where they outcompete and genetically swamp the Gray Duck, and they moved naturally to the Auckland Islands, where they are growing in number. Mallards introduced on the Falkland Islands apparently have not survived, but their status is still uncertain on the Kerguelen Islands.

The demise of whaling as a major southern seas industry and the reduced use of the great southern shipping route following construction of midcontinental canals markedly changed the role of humans in southern island ecosystems. But what of the future? Some islands, such as those owned by New Zealand, are faunal and floral preserves and presumably are safe from further settlements, mining, or industry. But with the pressures of human population, energy shortage, and growing need for food and natural products, the Antarctic Treaty is already being challenged. How intensively will exploration for oil or other minerals be pursued in the Antarctic? Will sealing or even whaling resume when these populations recover, since even southern fur seals are currently at harvestable levels? Will harvest of Antarctic fish and krill grow, since the Russians currently have had a research and experimental harvest program in international waters? Will commercial flights over the south pole become a reality, necessitating emergency airfields and support staff in remote southern outposts? Beyond these nearly predictable occurrences, what new endeavors will create further conflict between human needs and preservation of these delicate island systems.

A number of approaches are being used, and others should be developed to conserve island ducks and other unique island endemics. These are protection from unnecessary losses; habitat protection and management, including the provision for reliable food resources; control of exotic predators; avoidance of direct competitors; protection from abnormal human disturbance; and research to provide a base for understanding causes of population declines.

A number of islands are now completely protected by New Zealand, Australia, and the United States. In New Zealand, hunting is forbidden on Great Barrier Island, the last stronghold of the Brown Teal. Hunting restrictions are in force for all the U.S. island species, for the less common Falkland species, and for the South Georgia Pintail. Kerguelen Pintails are harvested but appear to be in no danger. Protection of the wintering area of migratory species like the Aleutian Canada Goose probably has contributed to reduced hunter kill.

Species surveys are regular (Laysan Teal) or periodic (Brown Teal and Auckland Flightless Teal) and provide a basis for understanding the degree of fluctuation in populations as well as determining dangerous levels. Facts are not available for island ducks in the areas of understanding production levels, food resources, and environmental limitations on breeding. No long-term studies of population survival and mortality have been undertaken, nor is information available on predation rates. Thus considerably more research is necessary. In some cases such research may have to be undertaken with great care, as with the small population of Laysan Teal. In other cases the number is sufficiently secure that slight mortality due to human activity is worth the resulting data base.

Controlling the spread of predators to smaller islets is extremely im-

Fig. 5.1. View from Adams Island across Victoria Passage to the main Auckland Island with a Wandering Albatross (*Diomedea exulans*) resting at lower right.

portant. Adams Island (Fig. 5.1), the second largest of the Auckland group, is one of the most pristine of southern islands and has never been seriously disturbed by humans or domestic livestock, but a few hundred meters across on the main Auckland Island feral pigs and cats exist. Monitoring of distributions and emergency control strategies are essential. Control of rats, cats, pigs, and mongooses has not, to my knowledge, been successful anywhere; new strategies are necessary for overcoming the impacts of such predators.

Fig. 5.2. Taro paddies at Hanalei National Wildlife Refuge, Kauai. Such paddies were established by ancient Polynesians and were undoubtedly used by Koloas then as they are today.

Habitat management of several types has been used to protect threatened waterfowl, but new approaches are essential. On Kauai construction of paddies for taro production by the early Polynesians undoubtedly influenced Hawaiian Duck numbers. These Koloas still use the paddies regularly, and the Hanalei National Wildlife Refuge uses them as the major management tool for Koloas as well as other endangered waterbirds (Fig. 5.2).

Control of damaging herbivores has been attempted in the Campbell Islands (sheep) and on the Galapagos Islands (goats), although neither has been directly related to duck populations. Removal of rabbits on Laysan resulted in recovery of the vegetation and subsequently the teal population, and goat control in Hawaii should protect the Nene's food and cover.

In extreme cases, totally artificial systems may be necessary until other problems such as efficient control of introduced predators are resolved. For example, I suspect that the Auckland Flightless Teal might use covered nest sites that could exclude pigs and even cats.

Transplants to islands not previously inhabited by the species is another possible strategy, but not all agree that this approach is either feasible or ethical, since it may disrupt another natural system and may endanger the few remaining individuals. Some work of this type has been successful with passerines in New Zealand, but a Laysan Teal transplant was unsuccessful (King 1973).

Captive breeding has been mentioned earlier in connection with several endangered island species. Kear and Williams (1978) summarized the threatened waterfowl and included the island species that have been successfully reared in captivity: the Nene, Laysan Teal, Brown Teal, Hawaiian Duck, and Aleutian Canada Goose. The Nene and possibly the Aleutian Canada Goose are increasing in number, seemingly because of reintroduction from captives on the breeding area and local predator control. Kear (1977) pointed out that the Laysan Teal will not become extinct as a race, since it can be reared so successfully in captivity, but that it could disappear as a wild bird. The question of genetic purity, ethical as well as biologically sound methods, and other issues relating to reintroduction of such species plague modern conservationists.

The "recovery team" approach used by the U.S. Fish and Wildlife Service endangered species program is an action approach to bring together knowledgeable people, synthesize data, and plan acquisition of data and habitat to ensure survival of the species. Such efforts now are under way for the Laysan Teal, Hawaiian Duck, Hawaiian Goose, Mariana Mallard, and Aleutian Canada Goose.

Because of their specialization for islands, island ducks are able to shift to increasingly smaller islands and islets until the size may provide a measure of the absolute limits of adaptation and the minimal needs of the species. Such islets tend to be the least disturbed, and this may explain why species survived there when they were absent on large islands (Auckland and Campbell flightless teal and Auckland Merganser). Complete and absolute protection of what may seem to be insignificant islets is therefore vitally important.

However, it is obvious from this and other studies that larger islands will attract and hold more species and probably provide greater population stability. The erratic population fluctuation of the Laysan Teal on its tiny home island may be an example of the tenuous relationship between population stability, environmental influence, and island size. Large island refuges are therefore vital to the preservation of both solitary endemic and island complexes, but these are more likely to be occupied and disturbed and more costly to acquire or protect. But the same principles apply to refuges designed for endangered waterfowl; for example, is it better to have one large refuge of taro patches on the island of

Kauai for Hawaiian Ducks, numerous small ones scattered about the island, clusters of small refuges, or a diversity of sizes? Although much discussed by various authors on a theoretical basis, there are no experimental data on which to base a survival plan for species that cling perilously to existence. This is a vital research need for the conservation of all species of wildlife but particularly for island species.

But new problems and new pressures seem to arise regularly for islands and island species. Ducks, like other island birds, may be indicators of our resource status. If our civilization reaches the state where we must exhaust the resources or destroy the natural biota of even these tiny islands, is there any hope for the preservation of anything natural? Will mankind learn to live with natural systems in a manner not destructive to all other species—or find themselves a relict on the tiny islets recently occupied by the last of the island ducks?

CHAPTER 6

Perspectives

DUCKS are a successful group of birds because they have adapted to habitats containing abundant food resources for which there seem to be few other avian competitors. A straining bill on a swimming or diving bird allows access to foods in wetlands ranging from puddles to deep open water. Variations on the general theme influence foraging success and habitat adaptability. Because aquatic flora and fauna are widespread (due in part to ducks), ducks tend to be less influenced by surrounding terrestrial vegetation and topography and adapt readily to various types of wetlands and habitats. Some ducks can feed in the uplands adjacent to water, and all geese do so.

The duck bill is an amazingly flexible food selector and sorter (Goodman and Fisher 1962), and modifications of the lamellae and nail optimize the bird for specific habitat resources. The evolution of the typical dabbling duck (genus *Anas*) probably was tied to an unstable habitat where various wetland types and fluctuating water conditions induced the use of various foods in diverse habitats. Such ducks have proved to be the optimal worldwide model. It is also logical that such an adaptable bird form is an excellent pioneer with flexibility in food resource and genetic systems.

Mobility is another characteristic of birds of unstable habitat, whether it is a product of climate (seasonality) or of fluctuating conditions (e.g., water levels). Seasonal migration is a result of annual temperature extremes at high latitudes where freeze-up is an annual event. Movements are more erratic and resource oriented where seasonality of rainfall is common as in the tropics, or irregular as in the desert. These incentives plus storm conditions and population expansion regularly result in pioneering. Many less mature island habitats with limited resources certainly must test the foraging ability of arriving pioneers. Many pioneers must perish there or depart for more productive habitats.

Selection in such habitats should favor smaller birds with more efficient food utilization balanced against proportionally greater heat loss of small bodies. Concurrent selection toward reduced extremities may further control heat loss and make a more wind-efficient and better adapted terrestrial bird. Smaller bill lamellae found in island ducks allow feeding on tiny invertebrates or seeds not usually consumed by ducks elsewhere.

Breeding ranges of ducks obviously are limited by the availability of the open water so essential to feeding. Wintering ranges in severe climates in the northern hemisphere also are limited to the northward by the availability of open water, usually along the seashore. Even in Greenland, Mallards are able to survive in open water along the seashore (Delacour 1956). While it is true that some wintering ducks like Mallards survive for some time in severe cold with only corn or other grains, most are held in such areas by the availability of warm water effluents or natural hot springs. Island geese that are forced to move out by severe winter weather tend to maintain a tight social structure and specific wintering areas, resulting in the formation of subspecies.

In the southern hemisphere certain species can overwinter at the tip of any continent because of the warmer climatic regime moderated by the sea. In South America many also migrate to less rigorous areas. However, migration from remote islands during periods of inclement weather is not feasible, and residents usually must survive at the seashore. It therefore seems that the southern range of resident ducks is limited by the northern extension of pack ice that would prevent feeding along the seashore. Whereas ducks survive on Kerguelen Island and South Georgia, none reside on the South Shetland, South Sandwich, and South Orkney islands, or on Heard Island, which are all enclosed by ice packs in winter.

The endemic tropical and subantarctic island ducks tend to be isolated and hence have more opportunity of developing species-level differentiation.

Pioneering on isolated, low-productivity islands provides a dramatic example of adaptability of an anatid in using many and diverse resources for survival. Such ecological expansion seems commonplace, and subsequent invasion by additional species must often meet failure because of the competition of island specialists. But island species tend to have low productivity rates evolved under stable conditions with less mortality. Pioneering species are often productive species; if a potential food resource can be exploited without severe competition, this high reproduction potential works in favor of their establishment. Following establishment, reproductive rates lessen with population stability as measured in clutch size and occasionally age of maturity and increased territoriality. Success of additions then is influenced by maturation of the system (i.e., greater productivity and habitat diversity) and by the segregation of potentially competing species in sharing of the resource. This process is the same as in more complex systems where greater species diversity is found, but each addition or deletion represents a greater proportionate change among waterfowl. Thus the evolution of fauna complexes is multifaceted.

Sexual dichromatism tends to be lost (or does not evolve) with the longer breeding periods in an ocean-moderated climate. Males may be in year-round attendance of females, and the less restricted breeding seasons reduce the competitive advantages of seasonally bright male plumages. Moreover, potentially increased predation rates may outweigh the advantages in sexual competition.

Current theories of island biogeography stress habitat limitations on island bird species richness (Lack 1969, 1976) versus the influence of size and distance and the equilibrium between species gains and losses (MacArthur and Wilson 1967). Observation during this study (yet to be quantified) suggests that habitat productivity and diversity are important influences on waterfowl survival and abundance in the often severe climate of islands. However, several examples suggest that size and occasionally distance also are strong influences on faunal development, periodic establishment and extinction are common, competitive interactions may be significant influences, and vacant niches may indeed occur. Thus the island ducks provide some further insights into the increasingly complex picture of island biogeography.

Island waterfowl need further study if they are to be preserved. All island systems seem sensitive to human influences and, historically, island flora and fauna have suffered severely. The understanding of simpler island systems can yield great insight into preservation and necessary management of habitats and species. Moreover, the concepts developed on island complexes are contributing greatly to our refuge and preserve strategies in larger and more complex systems (Diamond 1975).

Because of their adaptability to captivity, the island ducks can be captured, reared, and preserved in zoos and waterfowl collections; and this should be done. But their scientific uniqueness and role as indicators of environmental conditions warrant serious concern and effort toward preservation of island ducks in their natural habitat. Human influence undoubtedly will reduce the chances of success of many pioneers, and perhaps the evolution of unique characters in those that do succeed; but efforts toward maintaining naturalness of island systems will enhance preservation of present species and naturalness in future faunal dynamics.

LITERATURE CITED

Abbott, I., and P. R. Grant. 1976. Nonequilibrial bird faunas on islands. *Am. Nat.* 110(974):507-28.

Ali, S., and S. D. Ripley. 1968. *Handbook of the Birds of India and Pakistan,* vol. 1. Bombay: Oxford Univ. Press.

Amadon, D. 1943. Birds collected during the Whitney South Sea Expedition, 52. Notes on some non-passerine genera, 3. *Am. Mus. Novitates* 1237:1-22.

――――. 1966. Insular adaptive radiation among birds. In R. I. Bowman, ed., *The Galapagos,* proceedings of the symposium of the Galapagos international scientific program. pp. 18-20. Berkeley: Univ. Calif. Press.

American Ornithologists' Union. 1975. Report of the AOU Committee on Conservation, 1974-75. *Auk* 92(4):73.

――――. 1978. Proceedings of the ninety-fifth stated meeting, 22-26 August 1977, Berkeley, California. *Auk* 75(1) suppl.11AA.

Bailey, A. M. 1956. Birds of Midway and Laysan islands. *Denver Mus. Nat. Hist. Pictorial* 12:1-130.

Bailey, K. 1976. Potassium-argon ages from the Galapagos Islands. *Science* 192:465-67.

Baker, E. C. S. 1899. Indian ducks and their allies (pt. 6 with plate 6 of Andaman Teal). *J. Bombay Nat. Hist. Soc.* 12(2):235-61.

Baker, P. E., I. G. Gass, P. G. Harris, and R. W. LeMaitre. 1964. The volcanological report of the Royal Society expedition to Tristan da Cunha, 1962. *Phil. Trans. Roy. Soc. London,* Ser. A, 256(1075):439-578.

Baker, R. H. 1951. The avifauna of Micronesia, its origin, evolution, and distribution. *Univ. Kans. Publ. Mus. Nat. Hist.* 3:1-359.

Baldwin, P. H. 1945. The Hawaiian Goose, its distribution and reduction in numbers. *Condor* 47(1):27-37.

Balham, R. W. 1952. Grey and Mallard Ducks in the Manawatu District, New Zealand. *Emu* 52:163-91.

Balham, R. W., and K. H. Miers. 1959. Mortality and survival of Grey and Mallard Ducks banded in New Zealand. *N.Z. Dept. Intern. Aff. Wildl. Publ.* 1:1-56.

Ball, I. J., P. G. H. Frost, W. R. Siegfried, and F. McKinney. 1978. Territories and local movements of African Black Ducks. *Wildfowl* 29:61-79.

Bauer, K. M., and U. N. Glutz von Blotzheim. 1968. *Handbuch der Vögel Mitteleuropas,* vol. 2. Frankfurt am Main: Akademische Verlagsgesellschaft.

Beck, J. R. 1968. Unusual birds at Signy Island, South Orkney Islands, 1966-67. *Br. Antarct. Surv. Bull.* 18:81-82.

Beebe, W. 1924. *Galapagos: World's end.* New York: Putnam.

Bellrose, F. C. 1976. *Ducks, geese, and swans of North America.* Harrisburg, Pa.: Wildl. Manage. Inst. and Stackpole Press.

Bennett, A. G. 1920. Brevas notas sobre las aves antárticas. *Hornero* 2:25-34.

――――. 1922. Notas sobre aves sub-antárticas, I: Problemas que presenta la migración en algunas especies de aves sudamericanas. *Hornero* 2(4):255-57.

――――. 1926. A list of the birds of the Falkland Islands and dependencies. *Ibis* (12)2:306-33.

Berger, A. J. 1972. *Hawaiian birdlife.* Honolulu: Univ. Press Hawaii.

Biaggi, V. 1970. *Las aves de Puerto Rico.* Editorial Universitaria, Univ. Puerto Rico.

Bisset, S. A. 1976. Foods of the Paradise Shelduck *Tadorna variegata* in the high country of North Canterbury, New Zealand. *Notornis* 23:106-19.

Blaauw, F. E. 1916. Field notes on some of the waterfowl of the Argentine Republic, Chile, Tierra del Fuego. *Ibis,* Ser. 10, 4:478-92.

Bowman, R. I. 1960. *Report on a biological reconnaissance of the Galapagos Islands during 1957.* Paris: UNESCO.

Brock, V. E. 1951. Some observations on the Laysan Duck, *Anas wyvilliana laysanensis*. *Auk* 68:371–72.

Bryan, E. H., Jr., and J. C. Greenway. 1944. Contributions to the ornithology of the Hawaiian Islands. *Mus. Comp. Zool. Bull.* 94(2):80–142.

Bryan, W. A. 1901. *A key to the birds of the Hawaiian group.* Honolulu: Bishop Mus. Press.

Bryant, D. M., and J. Leng. 1975. Feeding distribution and behaviour of Shelduck in relation to food supply. *Wildfowl* 26:20–30.

Buller, W. L. 1873. *A history of the birds of New Zealand.* London: Van Voorst.

Burton, R. W. 1967. Stray birds at Signy Island, South Orkney Islands. *Brit. Antarct. Surv. Bull.* 11:101–2.

Butler, A. L. 1896. The oceanic teal (*Mareca*). *J. Bombay Nat. Hist. Soc.* 11:332–33.

Cabanis, J., and A. Reichenow. 1876. Uebersicht der auf der Expedition Sr. Maj. Schiff *Gazelle* gesammelten Vögel. *J. Ornithol.* 24:319–30.

Carrick, R. 1957. The wildlife of Macquarie Island. *Aust. Mus. Mag.* 12(8):255–60.

Cawkell, E. M., and the late J. E. Hamilton. 1961. The birds of the Falkland Islands. *Ibis* 103a(1):1–27.

Clapp, R. B., and P. W. Woodward. 1968. New records of birds from the Hawaiian Leeward Islands. *Proc. U.S. Nat. Mus.* 124(3640):1–39.

Clapp, R. B., and W. O. Wirtz. 1975. *The natural history of Lisianski Island, northwestern Hawaiian Islands.* Atoll Res. Bull. 186. Washington, D. C.: Smithsonian Inst.

Cody, M. L. 1966. A general theory of clutch size. *Evolution* 20:174–84.

_____. 1974. *Competition and the structure of bird communities.* Monogr. Pop. Biol. no. 7. Princeton, N.J.: Princeton Univ. Press.

Colinvaux, P. A. 1968. Reconnaissance and chemistry of the lakes and bays of the Galapagos Islands. *Nature* 219(5154):590–94.

Cooch, F. G. 1964. A preliminary study of the survival value of a functional salt gland in prairie Anatidae. *Auk* 81:380–93.

Cox, Allan. 1966. Continental drift in the southern hemisphere. In R. I. Bowman, ed., *The Galapagos,* proceedings of the symposium of the Galapagos international scientific program, pp. 78–86. Berkeley: Univ. Calif. Press.

Craig, D. A. 1974. Further information on the diet of the Blue Duck, *Hymenolaimus malacorhynchos. Mauri Ora* 2:137–38.

Delacour, J. 1954. *The waterfowl of the world,* vol. 1. London: Country Life.

_____. 1956. *The waterfowl of the world,* vol. 2. London: Country Life.

_____. 1959. *The waterfowl of the world,* vol. 3. London: Country Life.

_____. 1964. *The waterfowl of the world,* vol. 4. London: Country Life.

Delacour, J., and E. Mayr. 1945. The family Anatidae. *Wilson Bull.* 57(1):1–55.

Despin, B., J. L. Mougin, and M. Segonzac. 1972. Oiseaux et mammifères de l'Île de l'Est, Archipelago Crozet. *Comité national français des recherches antarctiques* 31:1–106.

Diamond, J. M. 1969. Avifaunal equilibria and species turnover rates on the Channel Islands of California. *Proc. Nat. Acad. Sci.* 64:57–63.

_____. 1972. *Avifauna of the Eastern Highlands of New Guinea.* Cambridge, Mass.: Nuttall Ornithol. Club no. 12.

_____. 1974. Colonization of exploded islands by birds: The supertramp strategy. *Science* 184:803–6.

_____. 1975. The island dilemma: Lessons of modern biogeographic studies for the design of natural reserves. *Biol. Cons.* 7:129–46.

Dobrowolski, K. A. 1969. Structure of the occurrence of waterfowl types and morphoecological forms. *Ekologia Polska,* Ser. A, 17(2):29–72.

Dunbar, M. J. 1968. *Ecological development in polar regions.* Concepts of Modern Biology Series. Englewood Cliffs, N.J.: Prentice-Hall.

Ealey, E. H. M. 1954. Ecological notes on the birds of Heard Island. *Emu* 54:91–112.

Edwards, I. S. 1955. The birds of Major Island. *Notornis* 6(4):118–19.

Eibl-Eibesfeldt, I. 1959. *Survey on the Galapagos Islands.* Paris: UNESCO.

Einarsen, A. S. 1965. *Black brant.* Seattle: Univ. Wash. Press.

Elliot, H. F. I. 1953. The fauna of Tristan da Cunha. *Oryx* 2:41–53.

Ely, C. A., and R. B. Clapp. 1973. *The natural history of Laysan Island, northwestern Hawaiian Islands.* Atoll Res. Bull. 171. Washington, D.C.: Smithsonian Inst.

Espenshade, E. B. 1970. *Goode's world atlas,* 13th ed. Chicago: Rand McNally.

Eyton, T. C. 1838. *A monograph of the Anatidae, or duck tribe.* London: Longman, Orme, Brown, Green, and Longman.

Fabricius, A. F. 1957. Climate of the subantarctic islands. In M. P. van Rooy, ed., *Meteorology of the Antarctic,* pp. 111–35. Pretoria, South Africa: Weather Bur., Dept. of Transport.

Falla, R. A. 1937. Birds. *B.A.N.Z. Antarct. Res. Exped., 1929–31,reps.* B(2):1–288.

———. 1953. The Australian element in the avifauna of New Zealand. *Emu* 53:36–46.

Falla, R. A., and E. F. Stead. 1938. The plumages of *Nesonetta aucklandica* Gray. *Trans. Roy. Soc. N.Z.* 68:37–39.

Falla, R. A., R. B. Sibson, and E. G. Turbott. 1967. *A field guide to the birds of New Zealand.* Boston: Houghton Mifflin and Cambridge: Riverside Press.

Federal Register. 1977. International trade in endangered species of wild fauna and flora. *Fed. Reg.* 42(35):10,461–88.

Finney, B. R. 1977. Voyaging canoes and the settlement of Polynesia. *Science* 196(4296):1277–85.

Fisher, H. I. 1965. Bird records from Midway Atoll, Pacific Ocean. *Condor* 67(4):355–57.

Fisher, W. K. 1903. *Birds of Laysan and the Leeward islands, Hawaiian group.* U.S. Fish Comm. Bull.

Fitzgerald, M. 1969. Some notes on the Paradise Shelduck. *Wildfowl* 20:69–70.

Fleming, C. A. 1962. History of the New Zealand land bird fauna. *Notornis* 9:270–74.

Fleming, J. H. 1935. A new genus and species of flightless duck from Campbell Island. *Occ. Papers Roy. Ontario Mus. Zool.,* vol. 1, no. 1.

Fosberg, F. R. 1966. The oceanic volcanic island ecosystem. In R. I. Bowman, ed., *The Galapagos,* proceedings of the symposium of the Galapagos international scientific program, pp. 55–61. Berkeley: Univ. Calif. Press.

Frith, H. J. 1967. *Waterfowl in Australia.* Honolulu: East-West Center Press.

Gadow, H. 1902. The wings and the skeleton of *Phalacrocorax harrisi. Tring Mus. Novitate Zool.* ix:169–76.

Gifford, E. W. 1913. Field notes on the land birds of the Galapagos Islands and of Cocos Island, Costa Rica. *Proc. Calif. Acad. Sci.,* pt. 1.,4(2):1–132.

Godwin, H., and V. R. Switsur. 1966. Cambridge University natural radiocarbon measurements. *Radiocarbon* 8:390–400.

Goodman, D. C., and H. I. Fisher. 1962. *Functional anatomy of the feeding apparatus in waterfowl.* Carbondale: S. Ill. Univ. Press.

Goodridge, C. M. 1839. *Narrative of a voyage to the South Seas and the shipwreck of the Princess of Wales cutter, with an account of two year's residence on an uninhabited island,* 6th ed. Exeter: author.

Gravatt, D. J. 1966. Ecological studies on the New Zealand Brown Teal (*Anas chlorotis*) on Great Barrier Island. Unpubl. undergraduate project, Univ. Auckland.

Gray, G. R. 1844. Birds in New Zealand. In *The geology of the voyage of HMS* Erebus and Terror, *under the command of Captain Sir James Clark Ross, R.M., F.R.S., during the years 1839–1843,* pp. 1–20. London: Janson.

Greenway, J. C., Jr. 1958. *Extinct and vanishing birds of the world.* Spec. Publ. 13. New York: Am. Comm. Intern. Wildl. Prot.

Greij, E. 1973. Effects of sex hormones on plumages of the Blue-winged Teal. *Auk* 90(3):533–51.

Gwynn, A. M. 1953. Some additions to the Macquarie Island list of birds. *Emu* 53:150–52.

Gyldenstolpe, N. 1955. Notes on a collection of birds made in the western highlands, central New Guinea, 1951. *Arkin f. Zool.,* Ser. 2, 8(1):1–181.

Hailman, J. 1977. *Optical signals.* Bloomington: Ind. Univ. Press.

Hall, R. 1900. Field-notes on the birds of Kerguelen Island. *Ibis* 21:1–34.

Hansen, H. A., and D. E. McKnight. 1964. Emigration of drought-displaced ducks to the Arctic. *Trans. N. Am. Wildl. Nat. Res. Conf.* 29:119–27.

Harris, M. 1974. *A field guide to the birds of the Galapagos.* London: Collins.

Henny, C. J. 1973. Drought-displaced movement of North American pintails into Siberia. *J. Wildl. Manage.* 37:23-29.

Heywood, R. B. 1967. The freshwater lakes of Signy Island and their fauna. *Phil. Trans. Roy. Soc. London,* Ser. B, 252(777):347-62.

Hitchcock, W. B. 1964. An introduction to the natural history of a New Guinea highland community. *Emu* 63(5):351-72.

Hochbaum, H. A. 1944. *The canvasback on a prairie marsh,* Washington, D.C.: Am. Wildl. Inst.

_____. 1946. Recovery potentials in North American waterfowl. *Trans. N. Am. Wildl. Conf.* 11:403-18.

Holdgate, M. W. 1960. Biology of the southern cold temperate zone. *Nature* 185(4708):204-6.

_____. 1967. The Antarctic ecosystem. *Phil. Trans. Roy. Soc. London,* Ser. B, 252(777):363-83.

Holdgate, M. W., and N. M. Wace. 1961. The influence of man on the floras and faunas of southern islands. *Polar Record* 10:475-93.

Horn, H. 1968. The adaptive significance of colonial nesting in the Brewers Blackbird (*Euphagus cyanocephalus*). *Ecology* 49:682-94.

Howard, H. 1975. Fossil anseriformes. In J. Delacour, ed., *The waterfowl of the world,* vol. 4, pp. 233-326, 371-78. London: Country Life.

Hume, A. O. 1873. *Mareca albogularis,* sp. nov. *Stray Feathers* 1(4):303-4.

Hume, A., and C. H. T. Marshall. 1880. *Game birds of India, Burma and Ceylon,* vol. 3. Calcutta.

Humphrey, P. S. 1955. The relationships of the sea-ducks (tribe Mergini). Unpubl. Ph. D. thesis, Univ. Mich., Ann Arbor.

Humphrey, P. S., and G. A. Clark, Jr. 1964. The anatomy of waterfowl. In J. Delacour, ed., *The waterfowl of the world,* vol. 4, pp. 167-232. London: Country Life.

Humphrey, P. S., D. Bridge, P. W. Reynolds, and R. T. Peterson. 1970. *Birds of Isla Grande (Tierra del Fuego).* Washington, D.C.: Smithsonian Inst.

Hutchinson, G. E. 1950. The biogeochemistry of vertebrate excretion. *Am. Mus. Nat. Hist. Bull.* 96:1-554.

Hutton, F. W. 1871. *Catalogue of the birds of New Zealand.* Wellington: Geol. Surv. N.Z.

_____. 1873. On geographical relations of the New Zealand fauna. *Trans. N.Z. Inst.* 5(1872):1-28.

Imber, M. J., and G. R. Williams. 1968. Mortality rates of a Canada Goose population in New Zealand. *J. Wildl. Manage.* 32(2):256-67.

International Council for Bird Protection. 1971. *Red data book,* vol. 2 (*Aves*). Morges, Switzerland: Intern. Union Cons. Nature Nat. Res.

Johnsgard, P. A. 1960. Hybridization in the Anatidae and taxonomic implications. *Condor* 62(1):25-35.

_____. 1965. *Handbook of waterfowl behavior.* Ithaca: Cornell Univ. Press.

_____. 1975. *Waterfowl of North America.* Bloomington: Ind. Univ. Press.

_____. 1978. *Ducks, geese and swans of the world.* Lincoln and London: Univ. Nebr. Press.

Johnson, A. W. 1965. *The birds of Chile,* vol. 1. Buenos Aires, S.A.: Platt Establ. Gráficos.

Johnston, D. W., and R. W. McFarlane. 1967. Migration and bioenergetics of flights in the Pacific Golden Plover. *Condor* 69:156-68.

Jones, H. L., and J. M. Diamond. 1976. Short-time-base studies of turnover in breeding bird populations on the California Channel Islands. *Condor* 78:526-49.

Jones, T. 1953. 1952 breeding results at Leckford. *Avic. Mag.* 59(1):8-12.

Kaplan, N. O. 1964. Lactase dehydrogenase—structure and function. *Brookhaven Symp. Biol.* 17:131-53.

Kear, J. 1970. The adaptive radiation of parental care in waterfowl. In J. J. Crook, ed., *Social behavior in birds and mammals,* pp. 357-92. London and New York: Academic Press.

———. 1973. The Blue Duck of New Zealand. *Living Bird* 11:175–92.

———. 1975. Salvadori's Duck of New Guinea. *Wildfowl* 26:104–11.

———. 1977. The problems of breeding endangered species. *Intern. Zoo Yearb.* 17:5–14.

Kear, J., and R. K. Murton. 1976. The origins of Australian waterfowl as indicated by their photoresponses. *Proc. Intern. Ornithol. Congr.* 16:83–97.

Kear, J., and R. J. Scarlett. 1970. Auckland Islands Merganser. *Wildfowl Trust Bull.* 21:78–86.

Kear, J., and T. H. Steel. 1971. Aspects of social behaviour in the Blue Duck. *Notornis* 18:187–98.

Kear, J., and G. Williams. 1978., Waterfowl at risk. *Wildfowl* 29:5–21.

Keith, K., and M. P. Hines. 1958. New and rare species of birds at Macquarie Island during 1956 and 1957. *CSIRO Wildl. Res.* 3(1):50–53.

Kidder, J. H. 1875. Ornithology. Contribution to the national history of Kerguelen Island. I. *U.S. Nat. Mus. Bull.* 2:1–51.

King, W. B. 1973. Conservation status of birds of central Pacific islands. *Wilson Bull.* 85:89–103.

Koskimies, J., and L. Lahti. 1964. Cold hardiness of the newly hatched young in relation to ecology and distribution in 10 species of European ducks. *Auk* 81:281–307.

Krapu, G. L. 1974. Foods of breeding Pintails in North Dakota. *J. Wildl. Manage.* 38:408–17.

Lack, D. 1947. *Darwin's finches.* Cambridge: Cambridge Univ. Press.

———. 1950. Breeding seasons in the Galapagos. *Ibis* 92:268–78.

———. 1954. *The natural regulation of animal numbers.* Oxford: Clarendon Press.

———. 1968. *Ecological adaptations for breeding in birds.* London: Methuen.

———. 1969. The number of bird species on islands. *Bird Study* 16(4):193–210.

———. 1970. Endemic ducks of remote islands. *Wildfowl* 21:5–10.

———. 1971. *Ecological isolation in birds.* Cambridge: Harvard Univ. Press.

———. 1974. *Evolution illustrated by waterfowl.* New York: Harper and Row.

———. 1976. *Island biology illustrated by the land birds of Jamaica.* Berkeley: Univ. Calif. Press.

Leopold, A. S. 1972. *Wildlife of Mexico.* Berkeley: Univ. Calif. Press.

Leveque, R. 1964. Notes sur la reproduction des oiseaux aux îles Galapagos. *Alauda* 32(1):5–44; (2):81–91.

Leveque, R., R. J. Bowman, and S. L. Billeb. 1966. Migrants in the Galapagos area. *Condor* 68(1):81–101.

Lönnberg, E. 1906. Contributions to the fauna of South Georgia. *K. Sven. Vet.-Akad. Handl.* 40(5):1–104.

———. 1920. The birds of the Juan Fernandez islands, 3. Zoology, pt. 1. In C. Skottsberg, ed., *The natural history of Juan Fernandez and Easter Island,* pp. 1–17. Uppsala.

Loranchet, J. 1915–16. Observations biologiques sur les oiseaux des Iles Kerguèlen. *Rev. Fr. Ornithol.* 4:113–16, 153–57, 190–92, 207–10, 240–42, 256–59, 305–7, 326–31.

Lorenz, K. 1951–53. Comparative studies on the behaviour of the Anatinae. *Avic. Mag.* 57:157–82; 58:8–17, 61–72, 86–94, 172–84; 59:24–34, 80–91.

Lowe, P. R. 1934. On the evidence for the existence of two species of steamer duck (*Tachyeres*) and primary and secondary flightlessness in birds. *Ibis* 4(13):467–95.

Lubbock, M. 1975. The Nene at home. *Wildfowl Trust Bull.* 72:11.

Lynch, J. F., and N. K. Johnson. 1974. Turnover and equilibria in insular avifaunas, with special reference to the California Channel Islands. *Condor* 76:370–84.

McAllum, H. J. F. 1965. The adaptation and increase in the Paradise Shelduck (*Tadorna variegata*) within a man-modified environment. *Trans. Roy. Soc. N.Z.* 6(12):115–25.

McArthur, P. D., and M. L. Gorman. 1978. The salt gland of the incubating Eider Duck *Somateria mollissima*: The effects of natural salt deprivation. *J. Zool.* 184:83–90.

MacArthur, R., and E. O. Wilson. 1967. *The theory of island biogeography.* Monograph in Population Biology 1. Princeton, N.J.: Princeton Univ. Press.

McGregor, R. C. 1905. *Birds from Mindoro and small adjacent islands.* Manila, P.I.: Dept Int., Bur. Govt. Lab.

McKinney, F. 1965. Spacing and chasing in breeding ducks. *Wildfowl Trust Ann. Rep.* 16:92–106.

Marshall, J. T., Jr. 1949. The endemic avifauna of Saipan, Tinian, Guam, and Palau. *Condor* 51(5):200–221.

Matthews, L. H. 1929. The birds of South Georgia. *Discovery Rep.* 1:561–659.

_____.1951. *Wandering albatross.* London: MacGibbon and Kee.

Mayr, E. 1931. Birds collected during the Whitney South Sea Expedition. XIII. *Am. Mus. Novitates* 486:1–29.

_____. 1942. *Systematics and the origin of species.* New York: Columbia Univ. Press.

_____. 1965. *Animal species and evolution.* Cambridge: Harvard Univ. Press (Belknap).

Mayr, E., and A. L. Rand. 1937. Results of the Archbold expeditions, no. 14. Birds of the 1933–1934 Papuan expedition. *Am. Mus. Nat. Hist. Bull.* 73:1–248.

Merilees, W. J. 1971. Bird observations—Macquarie Island, 1967. *Notornis* 18:55–57.

Miller, A. H. 1966. Animal evolution on islands. In R. I. Bowman, ed., *The Galapagos,* proceedings of the symposium of the Galapagos international scientific program, pp. 10–17. Berkeley: Univ. Calif. Press.

Moore, T. D. 1978. To the brink and beyond. *Audubon* 80(6):75–91.

Munro, G. S. 1944. *Birds of Hawaii.* Honolulu: Tongy.

Murphy, R. C. 1916. Anatidae of South Georgia. *Auk* 33:270–77.

_____. 1936. *Oceanic birds of South America,* vol. 2. New York: Macmillan and Am. Mus. Nat. Hist.

Navas, J. R. 1961. El pato de ala azul, *Anas discors,* capturado en la Argentina. *Neotropica* 7(23):52.

Newton, A. 1896. *A dictionary of birds,* pt. 4 (*Sheathbill-Zygodactyli*). London: Adam and Charles Black.

Oliver, W. R. B. 1955. *New Zealand birds,* 2nd ed. Wellington, N.Z.: Reed.

Olney, P. J. S. 1963. Interspecific diet differences in a group of sympatric Anatidae. *Proc. Intern. Congr. Zool.* 1:256.

Olrog, C. C. 1948. Observaciónes sobre la avifauna de Tierra del Fuego y Chile. *Acta Zool. Lilloana* 5:431–531.

_____. 1963. *Lista y distribución de las aves Argentinas.* Tucuman, Arg.: Univ. Nac. Tucuman, Instituto Miguel Lillo.

Olson, S. L. 1973. Evolution of the rails of the South Atlantic Islands (Aves: Rallidae). *Smithsonian Contrib. Zool.* 152:1–53.

Olson, S. L., and A. Wetmore. 1976. Preliminary diagnosis of two extraordinary new genera of birds from Pleistocene deposits in the Hawaiian Islands. *Proc. Biol. Soc. Wash.* 80:247–58.

Ornithological Society of New Zealand. 1953. *Checklist of New Zealand birds.* Wellington, N.Z.: Reed.

Osmaston, B. B. 1906. Notes on Andaman birds, with accounts of several species whose nests and eggs have not been hitherto described, pt. 2. *J. Bombay Nat. Hist. Soc.* 17:486–91.

Pagenstecher, H. A. 1885. Die Vögel Sud Georgiens nach der Ausbeute der Deutschen Polarstation in 1882 und 1883. *Jahrb. Hamb. Wiss. Aust.* 2:3–27.

Palmer, R. S. 1976a. *Handbook of North American birds,* vol. 2 (*Waterfowl,* pt. 1). New Haven and London: Yale Univ. Press.

_____. 1976b. *Handbook of North American birds,* vol. 3 (*Waterfowl,* pt. 2). New Haven and London: Yale Univ. Press.

Paulian, P. 1953. Pinnipedes, cetaces, oiseaux des Iles Kerguèlen et Amsterdam. Mission Kerguelen, 1951. *Mem. Inst. Sci. Madagascar,* Ser. A 8:111–234.

Perkins, R. C. L. 1903. *Fauna Hawaiiensis,* vol. 1 (*Vertebrate* pt. 4) London: Clay and Sons.

Phillips, J. C. 1923. *A natural history of the ducks,* vol. 2. London: Longman, Green.

Potts, T. H. 1870. On the birds of New Zealand. *Trans. Proc. N.Z. Inst.* 2:40–78.

Prevost, J., and J. L. Mougin. 1970. *Guide des oiseaux et mammiféres des terres australes et antarctiques française.* Paris: Dilochaus and Nestle.

Purdue, A. C. 1871. On a supposed new species of duck. *Trans. N.Z. Inst.* 4:213.

Rand, A. L. 1955. The origin of the land birds of Tristan da Cunha. *Fieldiana (Zool.)* 67:139–63.

Rand, A. L., and E. T. Gilliard. 1967. *Handbook of New Guinea birds.* London: Wiedenfeld and Nicolson.

Rand, A. L. and D. S. Rabor. 1960. Birds of the Philippine Islands. *Fieldiana (Zool.)* 35(7):223–441.

Rankin, N. 1951. *Antarctic isle.* London: Collins.

Reichenow, A. 1904. Neue Arten des Südpolargebiets. *Ornithol. Monatsber.* 12:46–47.

Reid, B., and C. Roderick. 1973. New Zealand Scaup *Aythya novae-seelandiae* and Brown Teal *Anas aucklandica chlorotis* in captivity. In N. Duplaix-Hall, ed., *International zoo yearbook*, no. 13, pp. 12–15. London: Zool. Soc. London.

Reischek, A. 1889. Notes on the islands to the south of New Zealand. *Trans. N.Z. Inst.* 21:378–89.

Richardson, F., and J. Bowles. 1964. A survey of the birds of Kauai, Hawaii. *Bishop Mus. Bull.* 227:1–51.

Ricklefs, R. E., and G. W. Cox. 1972. Taxon cycles in the West Indian avifauna. *Am. Nat.* 106:195–219.

Ridgeway, R. 1890. Scientific results of explorations by the U.S. Fish Commission Steamer *Albatross*, no. 1. Birds collected from Galapagos Islands in 1888. *Proc. U.S. Nat. Mus.* 11:101–5.

Ripley, S. D. 1942. A review of the species *Anas castanea. Auk.* 59:90–99.

———. 1957. The waterfowl of the world by J. Delacour (review). *Auk* 74:269–72.

———. 1960. Laysan Teal in captivity. *Wilson Bull.* 72(3):244–47.

Ripley, S. D., and G. M. Bond. 1966. The birds of Socotra and Abd al Kūrī. *Smithsonian Misc. Coll.* 151(7):1–37 and plates.

Ripley, S. D., and D. S. Rabor. 1958. Notes on a collection of birds from Mindoro Island, Philippines. *Yale Univ. Peabody Mus. Bull.* 13:1–82.

Robertson, C. J. R. 1976. The Campbell Island teal. *N.Z. Wildlife* 9:45–46.

Rothschild, W. 1893. *The avifauna of Laysan and the neighboring islands, with a complete listing to date of the birds of the Hawaiian possessions.* London: Porter.

Salomonsen, F. 1955. The evolutionary significance of bird-migration. *Dan. Biol. Medd.* 22(6):1–62.

———. 1976. The main problems concerning avian evolution on islands. *Proc. Intern. Ornithol. Congr.* 16:585–602.

Salvadori, T. 1894. Remarks on the ducks of the genus *Anas* and *Nyroca. Brit. Ornithol. Club Bull.* 20:1–2.

———. 1895. Order XIX, Chenomorphae. *Cat. Birds Brit. Mus.* 27:1–636.

Schwartz, C. W., and E. R. Schwartz. 1953. Notes on the Hawaiian Duck. *Wilson Bull.* 65(1):18–25.

Sclater, P. L., and O. Salvin. 1878. Reports on the collections of birds made during the voyage of HMS *Challenger. Proc. Zool. Soc. London* 10:576–79.

Scott, D., and J. Lubbock. 1974. Preliminary observations on waterfowl of western Madagascar. *Wildfowl* 25:117–20.

Scott, P. 1958. Notes on Anatidae seen on world tour. *Wildfowl Trust Ann. Rep.* 9:86–112.

———. 1960. BBC/IUCN Darwin centenary expedition. *Wildfowl Trust Ann. Rep.* 11:61–76.

Sibley, C. G. 1957. The evolutionary and taxonomic significance of sexual dimorphism and hybridization in birds. *Condor* 59:166–91.

Sibson, R. B. 1967. Speculating about shovelers near Auckland. *Notornis* 14(1):22–26.

Siegfried, W. R. 1970. Double wing-moult in the Maccoa Duck. *Wildfowl* 21:122.

———. 1974. Brood care, pair bonds, and plumage in southern Africa. *Wildfowl* 25:33–40.

Simberloff, D. 1976. Experimental zoogeography of islands: Effects of island size. *Ecology* 57(4):629–48.

Smith, R. I. 1968. The social aspects of reproductive behavior in the pintail. *Auk* 85:1–396.

Sowls, L. K. 1955. *Prairie ducks.* Harrisburg, Pa.: Wildlife Manage. Inst. and Stackpole.

Spenceley, G. B. 1958. The South Georgia Teal. *Wildfowl Trust Ann. Rep.* 9:196–98.

Storer, R. W., and F. B. Gill. 1961. El pato de ala azul, *Anas discors,* observado in la Provincia de Buenos Aires. *Neotropica* 7:92.

Stott, R. S., and D. P. Olson. 1973. Food-habitat relationship of sea ducks on the New Hampshire coastline. *Ecology* 54(5):996–1007.

Streets, T. H. 1877. Some accounts of the natural history of the Fanning group of islands. *Am. Nat.* 11(2):65–72.

Swanson, G. A., and H. K. Nelson. 1970. Potential influence of fish-rearing programs in waterfowl breeding habitat. In Symposium on the management of midwestern winterkill lakes, pp. 65–71. Spec. Publ. North Cent. Div. Am. Fish. Soc.

Swedberg, G. E. 1967. *The Koloa.* Preliminary report on the life history and status of the Hawaiian Duck (*Anas wyvilliana*). Honolulu: Dept. Land Nat. Res.

Szijj, J. 1965. Okologische Untersuchungen an Entenvögeln (Anatidae) des Ermatinger Beckens (Bodensee). *Die Vogelwarte* 23(1):24–71.

Terborgh, J., and J. Faaborg. 1973. Turnover and ecological release in the avifauna of Mona Island, Puerto Rico. *Auk* 90(4):759–79.

Thornberg, D. 1973. Diving duck movements on Keokuk pool, Mississippi River. *J. Wildl. Manage.* 37(3):382–89.

Tickell, W. L. N. 1965. New records for South Georgia. *Ibis* 107:388–89.

Todd, F. S. 1979. *Waterfowl: Ducks, geese and swans of the world.* San Diego: Sea World Press.

Udvardy, M. D. F. 1961. Unusual waterfowl observations. *Elepaio* 21:79–80.

Verrill, G. E. 1895. On some birds and eggs collected by Mr. George Comer at Gough Island, Kerguelen Island, and the island of South Georgia. *Trans. Conn. Acad. Arts. Sci.* 9:430–78.

Von der Steinen, K. 1890. Vogel auf Sud-Georgien. *In Die Deutschen Expeditionen und ihre Ergebnisse, Internationale Polarforschung, 1882–1883,* vol. 2, pp. 194–279. Berlin: Verlag von U. Usher.

Wace, R. H. 1921. Liste de aves de las Islas Falkland. *Hornero* 2(3):194–204.

Warham, J. 1969. Notes on some Macquarie Island birds. *Notornis* 16(3):190–97.

Warner, R. E. 1963. Recent history and ecology of the Laysan Duck. *Condor* 65:3–23.

Watson, G. E. 1975. *Birds of the Antarctic and subantarctic.* Washington, D.C.: Am. Geophys. Union.

Watson, G. E., R. L. Zusi, and R. E. Storer. 1963. *Preliminary field guide to the birds of the Indian Ocean (for use during the International Ocean Expedition).* Washington, D.C.: Smithsonian Inst.

Weller, M. W. 1968a. Notes on some Argentine anatids. *Wilson Bull.* 80:189–212.

————. 1968b. The breeding biology of the parasitic Black-headed Duck. *Living Bird* 7:169–207.

————. 1972. Ecological studies of Falkland Islands' waterfowl. *Wildfowl* 23:25–44.

————. 1974. Habitat selection and feeding patterns of Brown Teal (*Anas castanea chlorotis*) on Great Barrier Island. *Notornis* 21:25–35.

————. 1975a. Habitat selection by waterfowl of Argentine Isla Grande. *Wilson Bull.* 87:83–90.

————. 1975b. Notes on formation and life of ponds of the Falkland Islands and South Georgia. *Br. Antarct. Surv. Bull.* 40:37–45.

————. 1975c. Ecology and behaviour of the South Georgia Pintail *Anas g. georgica. Ibis* 117:217–31.

————. 1975d. Ecological studies of the Auckland Islands' Flightless Teal. *Auk* 92:280–97.

————. 1975e. Migratory waterfowl: A hemispheric perspective. In *Symposium on wildlife and its environment in the Americas.* Universidad Autonoma de Nuevo Leon Publ. Biolog. Inst. de Invest. Cient., 1(7):89–130.

————. 1976. Ecology and behaviour of steamer ducks. *Wildfowl* 27:45–53.

Weller, M. W., and R. L. Howard. 1972. Breeding of Speckled Teal *Anas flavirostris* on South Georgia. *Br. Antarct. Surv. Bull.* 30:65–68.

Wetmore, A. 1925. The Coues Gadwall extinct. *Condor* 27:36.

White, D. H., and D. James. 1978. Differential use of freshwater environments by wintering waterfowl of coastal Texas. *Wilson Bull.* 90:99–111.

Williams, G. R. 1962. Extinction and the land and freshwater-inhabiting birds of New Zealand. *Notornis* 10(1):15–24, 29–32.

_____. 1968. The Cape Barren Goose (*Cereopsis novae-hollandiae* Latham) in New Zealand. *Notornis* 15(2):66–69.

Williams, G. R., and M. W. Weller. 1974. Unsuccessful search for the Auckland Islands' Merganser (*Mergus australis*). *Notornis* 21:247–49.

Williams, H. 1966. Geology of the Galapagos Islands. In R. I. Bowman, ed., *The Galapagos,* proceedings of the symposium of the Galapagos international scientific program, pp. 65–70. Berkeley: Univ. Calif. Press.

Williams, M. J. 1970. Mallard/Grey hybridization. *N.Z. Wildlife* 2:47–48.

Williams, M. J., and C. Roderick. 1973. Breeding performance of Grey Duck (*Anas superciliosa*), Mallard (*Anas platyrhynchos*), and their hybrids in captivity. In N. Duplaix-Hall, ed., *International zoo yearbook* 13, pp. 62–69. London: Zool. Soc. London.

Wodzicki, K. 1965. The status of some exotic vertebrates in the ecology of New Zealand. In *The genetics of colonizing species,* pp. 425–60. New York: Academic Press.

Wolff, T. 1958. *The natural history of Rennell Island, British Solomon Islands,* vol. 1 (*Vertebrates*). Cophenhagen: Danish Scientific Press.

Wright, R. C., and D. Dewar. 1925. *The ducks of India.* London: Witherby.

Yamashina, Y. 1948. Notes on the Marianas Mallard. *Pac. Sci.* 11:121–24.

Yocum, C. F. 1964. Waterfowl wintering in the Marshall Islands, southwest Pacific Ocean. *Auk* 81:441–42.

I N D E X